THE

WINE MERCHANT'S MANUAL:

A TREATISE

ON THE

FINING, PREPARATION OF FININGS, AND GENERAL MANAGEMENT OF WINES,

BEING

THE RESULT OF FORTY YEARS' PRACTICAL EXPERIENCE IN
THE TREATMENT OF THE DIFFERENT WINES
CONSUMED IN THIS COUNTRY.

BY T. SMEED.

LONDON:

SMITH, ELDER AND CO., 65, CORNHILL.

1845.

London :
Printed by STEWART & MURRAY,
Old Bailey.

PREFACE.

THIS little Essay on the Treatment and Fining of Wines is presented to the trade, in the hope that it may prove generally useful both to the merchant and the cooper.

If there is one species of knowledge more essential to a wine merchant than another, it is a perfect acquaintance with the most wholesome, safe, and efficient treatment of his wines.

I should premise that this treatise is not the product of mere theory, or founded on other books on the subject, but is the result of above forty years' extensive and uninterrupted experience in the management of wines, aided by the instruction of which I had the advantage in early life from old practical coopers.

Without noticing the many systems which experience has exploded, or going further into the details of the manufacture of wines than is necessary to elucidate my system, I shall confine myself entirely to the treatment which wines require at the hands of the importer or merchant when they come into his possession ; and by explaining the nature, principle, and application of fining, and the mode of subduing the harsh and coarse qualities which are occasionally exhibited, to enable every merchant or his cellarman to pursue a safe, simple, wholesome, and certain mode of treatment, adapted to every variety of wines, under all circumstances.

It is also my object to show the benefit to be derived from attentive racking ; and the most efficacious method of discharging the colour of white wines, as well as to show the occasional expediency of blending wines, and give a few general hints necessary to be observed in the cellar.

CONTENTS.

ON

THE TREATMENT

AND

FINING OF WINES.

It is well known to those experienced in the trade, that the wines of the highest character are the produce of fruit favourably vintaged, after a propitious season, when the grapes have attained their full ripeness.

The culture of the grape and the making of wines are now conducted, in most countries, with greater attention than formerly; more care is generally bestowed on all that concerns the vintage, namely, in the selection of the grapes, at the gathering, the cleanliness of the vessels used in the fermentation, and in all the other details essential to the production of a clean and pure wine.

Notwithstanding the adoption of all these "means and appliances," we must not forget,

B

that, from the operation of various causes,—the nature of the soil, accidents of weather, or an unfavourable vintage,—an inferior quality of wine will sometimes be produced; and it is on the treatment necessary to the improvement and preservation of such wines that I shall presently offer the results of my experience.

It will generally be found that wines of the first class and character arrive in better condition, as regards appearance and retention of lee, than wines of inferior quality. It is also well known to merchants and men of experience, that pure and generous wines gradually ameliorate and develope their valuable properties without artificial aid, needing only a simple treatment, and an ordinary but efficient fining, to perfect their condition and brilliancy for bottling.

It will occasionally happen, when this class of wine is allowed to remain too long a time under finings, that a few flyers, or some light substance having too much buoyancy to remain long in adhesion to the subsided lee, after once fining, will ascend and become suspended again in the wine, in a greater or less degree. This will sometimes occur to an extent to render it prudent to rack the wine, in which case the repetition of a light fining becomes necessary; but it is very seldom that the finest description of wines requires to be subjected to any further process, provided that the finings used are properly prepared and applied.

The ordinary wines imported owe their character, in the first instance, much to the nature of the season, to the mode adopted in the vintage and manufacture, and to other contingencies, on which I shall have frequent occasion to remark.

Such is the difference arising from the nature of the grape, soil, and climate, that some wines will readily deposit their tartarous qualities, whilst other wines will retain them in suspension; and, when the latter is the case, the development of their more generous properties becomes retarded, and the influence of the unfavourable quality disengaged, deprives the wine of its chance of amelioration. It is on such an occasion that the skill of the merchant or cooper is called into requisition, in order to the extraction of the quality so inconsistent with vinous purity. A fining efficacious to the remedy of this defect has long been a desideratum with all who are concerned in the management of wines. Many kinds and qualities of wine, when coming into the hands of the importer or merchant, require a specific fining for the complete liberation of those noxious qualities: this can only be accomplished by the application of suitable finings, combined with the process of racking. This system is absolutely essential to render such wines clean and fit for consumption.

Now, as regards wines that are free from such defects, we know that it is attributable to the due balance of the desirable constituent properties present in the fruit, when subjected to the press, combined with the care and skill required to be exercised in the process of fermentation. The grower, or factor, when these advantages are secured, is enabled to produce a pure, perfect, and grateful wine. The shipper, importer, or merchant, has only then to apply an ordinary fining, properly prepared, to effect the perfect condition of such wines.

When the merchant takes into his stock any quantity of wine intended for immediate consumption, of whatever description, the process of fining follows, as a matter of course; and he administers himself, or leaves to the cellarman to administer, such fining, and in such proportion, as he deems necessary to perfect the subsidence of lee, and expecting, doubtless, to insure the brilliancy of the wine, and to improve, as far as possible, its general condition. After a reasonable time allowed for that purpose, he probably finds it bright, and from the apparent brightness and condition of the wine, the merchant will deter-

mine on the expediency of bottling it, as occasion
may require. Relying upon the quality of the
finings used, he calculates on a continuation of
the brilliancy of the wine bottled; and supposing
the finings to have been appropriate, and due
attention to have been bestowed on it in other
respects, he will, so far, have performed his duty.
But supposing that, at no distant period, flyers
make their appearance in the wine, or it exhibits
a dulness, or probably becomes gradually cloudy,
and ultimately foul, to what cause will it be attributable? Such a result has very frequently been
a subject of complaint, and it not only brings
discredit on the merchant, but is often attended
with serious inconvenience and loss. It is quite
evident that this must arise from mismanagement
in some shape or other, or from the inefficiency of
the fining applied, and occasionally to both of
these causes.

Important, however, as is due attention in the
treatment of wines, much depends on the efficiency of a fining, and that efficiency depends on
the preparation of it. Every person concerned
in the management of wines-knows that isinglas is the principal ingredient used, and that
it is the most pure and appropriate of ordinary
finings for white wines, when properly prepared.
But the system that has been, and is at the pre-

sent time, adopted by many, of dissolving isinglas for *wine finings,* is far from being proper. The mode most efficacious and practically applicable to all white wines has long occupied the attention of the trade. The system adopted in many instances has been found but partially effective, and that even when the isinglas has been proved to be of the finest quality, which sufficiently demonstrates a defect in preparation. Various plans are followed both by the fining-makers and the merchants who make their own. A great proportion of the finings vended is made with strong acidulous liquids variously compounded. These acids do not form the basis essential to the completion of a fining, so as to render its action effective and incorporate the matter precipitated with the subsided lee,—a result indispensable to the brilliancy of the wine. In fact, these compositions in some instances operate quite adversely, and are decidedly objectionable on account of the abominable odour which they emit, and with which wines have in many instances become imbued. The frequent failures ensuing from the use of finings thus improperly compounded sufficiently prove the fallacy of many of the systems pursued. The subject is one of the utmost importance to every one concerned in the trade, and if a uniform system can be pointed out (which I propose to do) for the preparation of a fining perfectly simple in its properties, and efficacious and practically applicable to all *white wines*, the advantages would be unquestionable. The main point to be regarded in the formation of a fining for all description of white wines, is the action of precipitation upon, and combination with, certain particles suspended in the wine, indispensable to secure stability of lee—a process essential to the permanent brilliancy of white wines.

In the course of my remarks, I shall have frequent occasion to advert to the mode of preparing finings, in order that every one may clearly understand the relative properties and true constituents of a fining.

Without, of course, asserting that there is no system of fining at present in use which is not objectionable, I have no hesitation in affirming, that the true principle in the preparation of finings is very imperfectly practised, and that the mode generally pursued is very defective.

The objects to be regarded, as I have already observed, in the preparation of a *fining* from *isinglas*, is the intrinsic purity, sympathy, and coexisting principle of the ingredients used in dissolving the isinglas;—secondly, the steady action of the fining in effecting the precipitation of the suspended particles present in wines, and their permanent adherence to the sediment when completely formed into lee. These are qualities indispensable in the preparation of a *fining*, to which alone we can look for the maintenance of the brilliancy of wines. The method employed by many is founded upon principles the very reverse of these, and in some instances operates injuriously upon the quality of the wine. Many of the ingredients used in the dissolving process absolutely tend to the dissolution of the lee; in fact, the modes often resorted to are in every respect futile,—the invention of some idle habit; they serve no real object, and yet they are used by persons who are too careless to inquire into the subject, and who are probably wholly incapable of assigning any reason for the results.

It must, I imagine, be very evident to any person of ordinary experience, that the condition, amelioration, and preservation of wine in bottle, depend wholly on the degree of its previous condition and maturity in wood, and to the perfect freedom from all detrimental particles which it might at any time have held in suspension. It is highly necessary that this fact be borne particularly in mind, the brilliancy of wines in bottle being wholly dependent on it.

Every cooper and cellarman of experience, who has watched the action, progress, and ultimate re-

sults of finings, variously prepared, must admit
the impropriety of dissolving isinglas with strong
acids, stale cyder, and other powerful acidulous
liquids. I admit that the isinglas may readily
be dissolved with such compounds, and that the
brilliancy of the wine may apparently be perfected; but in nineteen instances out of twenty
the wine so fined and bottled becomes, at no distant period, flyery or foul. If we introduce in the
composition of a fining any ingredient possessing,
in however small a degree, the fermentative principle, we immediately hazard the steadiness of the
lee, which is readily acted upon by any fermentative
application; and thus a reaction takes place in the
sediment formed, and the lee becomes disturbed.
Consequently, what one part of the fining perfects,
the other subverts ; in which case, the lighter
particles of subsided matter, from their natural
buoyancy, separate and ascend, and we perceive
the particles floating in the wine. Thus it is with
wine when it assumes a dull or cloudy appearance
after having once attained brilliancy : the defect is
generally attributable to one and the same cause.

It must, I think, be manifest to those who
well consider this subject, that a very essential
and important point in the preparation of an ordinary fining for white wines, is the fitness of the
ingredients used in dissolving the isinglas; its

coefficient influence on the precipitant substances, in causing their permanent incorporation with the sedimental lee. These relative principles must exist in the composition of a perfect fining ; and, as I have already observed, it is only by a fining combining these affinities and immutable properties, that we are enabled to effect the condition and brilliancy of wines, with a certainty of their retaining that condition for any length of time after being bottled.

I have already mentioned, that it is not my design to dwell upon the manufacture of wines; but in order satisfactorily to enter upon the merits of the treatment applicable to the different varieties, it is absolutely necessary to notice the cause of the difference of quality. I shall merely make such allusions as will enable me to explain my views upon certain points relative to the necessity for the variation of finings ; and I feel convinced that I shall be enabled to lay down a system that shall be applicable under all circumstances, and to all descriptions of wines.

Now, for example, we know that the purity, and every other desirable property of wine, are owing, in the first instance, to the state of soundness, maturity, and perfection of the grape, and to the abundance of the saccharine property present when submitted to the press : yet the saccharine principle will remain inactive, unless it is combined with other natural qualities in quantity sufficient to cause that mysterious change necessary to perfect the fermentation. The second essential for a pure and perfect wine, is the judicious mode pursued and the attention exercised in the fermentation. Thus the factor or shipper is enabled on these favourable occasions to obtain such wines in a state of purity; and here we arrive at a point to which I am desirous of drawing the especial attention of my reader. For the sake of illustration, we will suppose that a portion of such wine has been received, and found to be a clean, pure, generous wine. In this case we have only to follow one general rule as regards the fining; assuming that they are white wines, we need but the finest quality of isinglas, appropriately prepared (the direction for which will be found in another part of this little work) to effect their perfect condition and brilliancy; and, in the other case, we require but the white of fresh eggs for red wines of a like good quality.

Now, as regards the treatment of this quality of wines, there can be no difficulty in deciding on the preferable mode; namely, the most simple. The necessity of properly preparing the isinglas, to render the fining efficacious, must be borne in mind.

It may not be thought out of place if I here hint at the propriety of securing, after a particularly fine vintage, as large a portion of the wine as may be convenient. I think it will be admitted that the import and shipping houses of respectability are always willing to afford the merchant every facility on such an occasion. At all events, it behoves the merchant to be alive to the advantages of securing a portion of the wines, exceeding his immediate wants, for many obvious reasons; one (the most prominent) of which is the value of such wines in blending and bringing up other wines wanting character, probably the produce of a less favourable vintage. There are many circumstances under which the blending of wines, when skilfully managed, becomes as satisfactory to the consumer as it is advantageous to the merchant.

The respectable shipping houses and foreign correspondents invariably endeavour every season, and particularly on the occasion of a favourable vintage, to procure a portion of the choicest wines commensurate with their expectation of orders for shipment; and it is obviously their interest to bestow such attention on these wines, both previously to, and at the time of, shipment, as shall render them as clean as possible, and thereby ensure their progression to maturity and the development of their vinous properties; thus leaving little for the future management of the importer or merchant. When these results are satisfactory, and the merchant is convinced the wines have been properly treated, he has only to apply an ordinary fining to perfect the condition of that wine, when intended for the bottle. In order to perform this necessary operation with success, the merchant's first care should be to place the wine in a situation the temperature of which is suited to its character : this is a point very essential in promoting the perfect and permanent brilliancy of the wine. It is then equally important that the finings be pure, appropriate, and judiciously applied : all this being effected, the merchant may look forward to the attainment of the object desired.

Much might be said of the great advantages which the opulent and influential houses possess over others less fortunate ; but as such advantages are, I presume, generally familiar to the trade, it would be useless to lengthen this treatise by dwelling upon them. We know that particularly good vintages do not often follow in quick succession ; that the most opulent houses, notwithstanding their anxious endeavours to procure and ship their wines in the most perfect condition, are occasionally to some extent, from unavoidable accidents, foiled in their object, especially in the

event of a succession of unfavourable vintages.
The full, fruity, pure wines retained in store,
adapted for blending, have probably become exhausted, which leaves but one obvious alternative
to the shipper.   To this point he directs his operations, and applies the most judicious treatment
his means afford for the general improvement of
the wines intended to be shipped.   However, in
seasons unfavourable to the vintage, the merchant
must expect to find some portion of the wines
short of perfection ; the tartarous and other qualities opposed to the vinous properties exist more
abundantly.   This defect, after the voyage and
the allowance of a little time for maturing, may
in a great measure be remedied.   There are means
simply and conveniently applicable, which it is
unquestionably expedient for the merchant to
adopt for the amelioration and preservation of
such wines.

It is not so much to the species of vine itself, as
it is to the nature and quality of the soil and
climate in which the grape grows, that wines owe
their peculiarities of flavour, fragrance, and general
excellence.   Nevertheless, the productions of these
favoured spots are not invariably exempt from
the common accidents that frequently operate
unfavourably both on the vine itself and the product.   Despite the care of the cultivator, canker

and several other diseases frequently affect the vine, and the unfavourableness of a season acts prejudicially on the grape; indeed, the accidents tending to the deterioration of the fruit in its progress to maturity are innumerable. When the grape becomes affected from any of these natural causes, the injury, as a matter of course, extends to the produce of the press, however careful and judicious may have been the management of the frabricator.

Now, on the arrival, or reception into store, of any wines little or much affected from the causes just referred to, the propriety of submitting them to a simple and wholesome process of fining will not be disputed. Indeed, all wines that exhibit any defects on their arrival ought to be subjected to this process, and then carefully racked; for this simple reason, that, as the wine gains age, it naturally continues to precipitate its extraneous particles, and, at proper periods in its progress to maturity, we are enabled, by an appropriate auxiliary fining, with the ordinary fining of isinglas or eggs, and judicious treatment in other respects, to assist and finally complete the subsidence of all superfluous matter, and thus enhance the purity and wholesomeness of the wine.

We know that wines, the product of fruit that has imbibed any obnoxious quality, are, after

undergoing fermentation, chiefly dependent for
their future character on judicious management
during their progress to maturity.   If, therefore,
we find, on the arrival of wines, or on receiving
them into stock, that this important process has
been neglected, and that there is a predominance
of some quality opposed to the vinous property,
it unquestionably becomes the duty of the importer or merchant to adopt the means necessary
to free such wines as far as possible from the
objectionable quality.

It may here be observed, that, although this has
been a subject which has engaged the attention of
most persons in the wine trade, it is acknowledged
that the system pursued for thus correcting and
improving the flavour of wines, has been generally
inefficient to the end purposed, the finings usually
employed having been unsuitable to the purpose.

It must be very evident, that before any permanent improvement can possibly be effected in
wines possessing any degree of coarseness, harshness, &c., we must remove, by an appropriate
fining, the existing defects; then, by carefully
racking the wine, we separate it from all objectionable matter which it previously retained in
suspension, thus affording the vinous properties the power of development.   It will not be
improper here to impress on the mind of the

young cooper, that wines which have not fully deposited their impurities will invariably improve from the operation of careful racking after the application of efficient finings ; in fact, it is the only system practically applicable for the attainment of their ultimate condition. I may also, before I proceed further, urge upon him the expediency of performing these operations with all wines of ordinary and inferior quality, whether designed for bottling or blending. If intended for bottling, they invariably require to be once or twice properly fined and carefully racked, otherwise they seldom retain their brilliancy ; and if intended for blending, the cleaner we can get them the better.

If, in the fabrication of wines, there should be a deficiency of the saccharine property, a generous wine will not be produced ; but if the saccharine property, and other essential qualities present in the grapes when submitted to the press, should be tolerably proportioned, the fruit moderately free from decay and extraneous matter, a good ordinary wine will be the result. When the saccharine property proves abundant in the grape, and the fruit itself is pure and free from defect, a wine possessing the highest qualities and character will be produced, if proper attention be exercised in the fermentation.

When inequalities in the saccharine property and other vegetable qualities necessary to produce fermentation occur, different results will be exhibited. When there is a deficiency of the saccharine property, and a predominance of any quality foreign to the vinous purity, in the grapes when submitted to the press, the result will be the production of inferior wines, varying in quality proportionably to the foreign matter with which the fruit became charged. We know that *sugar*, *tartarous* and *malic acid*, *vegetable extract*, and *aqueous matter*, are the ingredients in the composition of the grape; and, as I have already observed, according as these qualities vary in quantity in the fruit previous to its conversion into wine, different results are produced. Hence arises the variety in the qualities of wines.

Now, if we admit the existence of defectiveness in the grape, even in a slight degree, previously to its conversion into wine, we need no great argument to show that a corresponding defectiveness will be exhibited in wines after their having completed their fermentation. Experience sufficiently proves, that the quality opposed to the production of a pure wine does not readily disengage itself by free deposits, and when left suspended in wines it deprives them of their proper flavour. Moreover, the same defects will be discoverable in the wine

in bottle, and will prove as injurious to its preservation as it will to its appearance.

It is to the treatment of the ordinary, or what
may be termed the second and third class wines,
that I shall now proceed to advert; and here it
may not be amiss to observe, that the casual
shippers frequently send off their wines before
they have had sufficient time to deposit their
impurities; in short, wines are shipped in different stages of condition, and it is principally
from this cause that we meet with so many various qualities of wines in the market.

As regards the treatment of the ordinary or
coarse description of wines, I need scarcely observe, that the adaptation of a fining for remedying
the defects I have adverted to, has engaged the
attention of every practical man concerned in the
management of wines; but to attempt to enu-
merate one-half the ingredients that have been
employed, the mode of preparation and application, would be as tedious as it is unnecessary; I
shall therefore content myself by a brief reference
to what has commonly been used;—thus, prepared chalk or lime has been applied previously to
the use of the ordinary finings, in the proportion of
half a pound or a pound to a pipe or butt of wine.
Various calcined earths have been similarly applied; Spanish earth and prepared chalk mixed

together, in the proportion of a pound of the for-
mer to half a pound of the latter, have also very
frequently been used to a pipe or butt of wine;
but the chief advantage of this mixture is found
in its application to wines that have become
scuddy, in which single instance its use is not only
not improper, but will generally be found to produce the desired effect, particularly in such wines
as may be affected from their having been
transported in skins.   Gypsum and similar ingredients have been, and are now, used in various
ways; but I hold them to be utterly unsuited to
the purpose.   In some countries a sort of lime-
stone is obtained, which, when baked and pul-
verized, is employed occasionally with some little
advantage.   However, these methods generally
fail in producing the full effect desired; their
advantages are but partial, and the use of them is
often more injurious than beneficial.   Their earthy
qualities render them generally inappropriate, and
constitute a grave objection to their adoption.
Without retorting upon the advocates of these
old practices (assuming they have been pursued with the best intentions), I must express my
conviction, that they have often been employed
by persons ignorant of the true principle of treatment.

What we have first to regard in a fining is its
freedom from any peculiar smell or flavour, as it

is very evident that those qualities will be communicated to the wine; and although this may rarely be detected, it will at all times be prudent to bear in mind the precaution, especially in the case of delicate wines. Secondly, the power of the materials of which the fining is composed, to effect the entire subsidence of the obnoxious substances. Thirdly, its stability when in combination with the sedimental lee, so essential to perfect and complete the brilliancy of the wine. Now, with regard to the ordinary and inferior class of wines, we have, in most instances, two objects in view,—the riddance of all objectionable qualities, in order to get them into the best possible state of condition in wood previously to showing them for sale, &c.; and the retention of their brilliancy.

The treatment necessary to the improvement of the ordinary and inferior quality of wines, is to some, I am aware, but a secondary consideration. To the holders, however, of such wines, it is obviously a matter of importance, and one which is well worth their attention. I shall here make a few observations upon the action of the usual finings of isinglas and the whites of eggs, and, at the same time, point out an auxiliary, really efficacious and practically applicable, for the improvement and preservation of this class of wines.

Its peculiar operation in connection with isinglas or eggs, together with its purity, renders it eminently adapted to the purpose. However, as on this subject, as well perhaps as on others, prejudice often prevails over thorough experience, some of my readers may differ from my views; I shall, nevertheless, freely give my opinion on the mode of treatment for which I contend, and which is founded upon long practical experience. It is well known to all those conversant with the management of wines, that isinglas or the white of eggs is admirably adapted, when properly prepared, for finings for all kinds of wines, and all-efficient for wines possessing intrinsic purity. It must, at the same time, be allowed, that neither the one nor the other has much influence on that extraneous and tartarous quality to which the occasional coarseness and harshness exhibited in wines are attributable.

I presume it will be admitted, that it is both prudent and expedient to free such wines as have retained in a greater or less degree the unfavourable qualities derived from the grape, from the defects already adverted to. It must, I think, be evident, that if such obnoxious qualities are not worked out in the course of fermentation, or corrected shortly after the completion of that process, the wine cannot possibly progress or improve in flavour; but if left to remain in that state, it gradually deteriorates, from the influence of those noxious matters imperceptibly suspended in it. Now, in these instances of coarseness, harshness, or other incidental defects in wines, isinglas or the white of eggs has this beneficial effect, as it has upon all sorts of wine: it assists the precipitation of such matter, perfects the compactness of the lee formed; and this is the extent of its influence. There is no property in either the one or the other tending to neutralize or correct the exciting quality of the coarseness and other defects in wines.

That both are admirably adapted for finings for all qualities of wines is indisputable. Nevertheless, if an auxiliary ingredient intrinsically wholesome can be brought in to operate upon, and to remedy to a considerable extent, the defects adverted to, surely the expediency of its adoption will be obvious; and here it may be remarked, that were this system more generally acted upon before the symptoms of decay become apparent, a greater portion of the ordinary wines would leave their bonded habitations. We are well aware, that, notwithstanding the attention bestowed by the cultivator and factor, a portion of ordinary wines will unavoidably be produced, the quantity and quality being dependent on the in-

fluence of the season. Those who are familiar
with the trade know also that wines from various
causes are frequently shipped in an imperfected
state. The amelioration of wine depends invariably upon the presence of foreign matter in contact with it; therefore I contend that such wines
as have been more or less affected by any unfavourable quality existing in the grape, and
transmitted to its produce, require and deserve, at
the hands of the importer or merchant on their
coming into their possession, a large share of their
attention, and that much may often be done in
way of improvement by a judicious mode of
treatment.

From the preceding remarks it will be obvious,
that, if we possess any means of remedying these
casual defects, by converting the obnoxious matter into a perfect subsidence of lee, and, by thus
separating the wine from it, we preserve and enhance its wholesomeness, it is our own fault if we
do not take advantage of the system. Now long
and careful investigation has discovered a means
of perfectly accomplishing this purpose; the method is acknowledged by those who have adopted
it to be based upon the soundest principle, and
those scientifically experienced have pronounced it
to be unsurpassed in certainty and simplicity.

All those substances which we find diffused in

wines that form what may be termed the natural
lees, are easily separated by the finings prepared
with isinglas, or with the aid of the whites of
eggs; simply for this reason, the predisposition of
these substances to separate and precipitate themselves, renders it merely necessary that they be
combined with heavier matter to effect their total
subsidence. But if it be borne in mind that the
noxious quality causing pungency and other defects in wines, to which allusion has been particularly made, is retained principally in an incorporated and undecomposed state of fluidity, and
diffused through the whole body of the wine; it
will be evident that an auxiliary fining, specifically
calculated to disunite the obnoxious matter, is not
only a desideratum, but absolutely indispensable.
Pre-eminently adapted to this purpose is the CON-
CRET MARIN.

The *concret marin* is by no means a new preparation, it being well known to a few. It is
composed of marine shells, of which there are some
peculiarly adapted to the purpose; but the vast
improvement that has recently been effected in
the sublimation of this article has originated in
my suggestions, the result of much consideration,
and several experiments on the subject.

Where the *concret marin* is brought into use, it
will establish a uniform mode of treatment with

D

all those wines that are in any degree affected by the causes referred to. "The concrete cannot possibly be surpassed for its intrinsic purity. It is more tasteless than isinglas or eggs, and the little fragrancy it possesses is decidedly preferable to either. In every instance in which I have used the concrete, in its present state, I have succeeded in perfectly divesting wines of the coarseness and other qualities opposed to their true flavour, being assisted of course by the ordinary finings, combined with attention and cleanliness in the operation of racking, so needful on these occasions. The favourable influence which the concrete has on wines may be perceived in a few days.

I trust I may not be thought presumptuous, if I here refer to a complimentary remark, in a letter I received from a merchant in the vicinity of Bordeaux, who, in the autumn of 1843, possessed a considerable stock of vin de grave, which, for the most part, assumed an unfavourable character, and continued in a very indifferent condition. He had solicited my advice as to the best mode of treatment to be adopted. His letter is dated last October :—

" With respect to the application of the method you were kind enough to advise me to pursue with my vin de grave last autumn, I am happy to inform you that it answered exceedingly well.

I succeeded in perfecting their condition completely, and they improved much beyond my expectation, and, as you justly observed, I have found the adoption equally advantageous in other wines; indeed it has yielded most excellent results, which to me have been of great importance."

The *concret marin* is applied with the greatest advantage to wines, as it is peculiarly adapted to counteract and neutralize all acescency, a material point in the treatment of those of the ordinary class. I am aware there have been many absurd and ridiculous ingredients employed occasionally for various objects, and regarded by some as great secrets. I could specify sufficient to fill a volume, but it would be a waste of time, and foreign to my purpose. The instructions contained in this little work are intended to render the management of wines easy to all connected with the trade; to propound a system free from intricacy and infallible in practice, and guided by which the merchant may ensure the preservation of his wines, and prevent or remedy the various accidents to which they are liable.

I have endeavoured in my preceding remarks to describe the action of a fining, and the necessity for its modification to the different qualities of wines; I shall here make a few observations upon the well-known fact of wines becoming *flyery*, cloudy, or foul, both in wood and bottle, after having been fined and become bright. The real cause in some instances is not easily to be defined. I freely confess it has often puzzled me to account for it; when, however, it does happen, it operates to the annoyance of the merchant in a variety of ways; and when occurring to wine in bottle, after being sent out, will, of course, injure his reputation with the consumer; indeed, the inconvenience and loss accruing to the merchant from such occurrences on some occasions, are very serious. It is a subject to which the young cooper, or any person desiring to become skilled in the management of wines, ought particularly to devote much of his attention.

I may, perhaps, differ from some of my readers on the causes of these accidents; however, I shall candidly express my opinion on the subject, and explain the method I have adopted to obviate them. It must often have been observed by most merchants and coopers of experience, that *flyers* have occasionally appeared and afterwards disappeared in wines in wood, after they had attained a tolerable brightness from the fining applied. To precisely account for the cause of this disturbance of lee on all occasions would be next to impossible; but I think it may in general be pretty accurately explained. There is no question that these incidents may be often traced to the fact of sufficient time not having been allowed for the disengagement and deposit of the particles generally present in wines. I need not, I presume, in order to make this evident, instance the different wines that continue for a lengthened period to make deposits in various degrees. The nature of the grape, soil, and season, may be regarded as having something to do with it. We may take the single instance of port wines: there have been many disputes as to the number of years port wines will continue to deposit the matter which forms the crust; the same reasoning is in a measure applicable to many other kinds of wines. I have known, as have no doubt most experienced merchants and coopers, some of the most highly esteemed white wines, to form in various degrees, crust on the bottles. I can cite two instances in particular, of the finest Madeira and white Burgundy that I ever met with, and for which the most extravagant price might have been obtained, having formed a complete crust ;— that of the Madeira a perfect buff colour, and that of the Burgundy a shade lighter. The crust so formed in both instances adhered to the bottle so firmly that the wine was decanted perfectly bright to the last drop. Now, how shall we

account for it? It is true I have heard many
theories on these and similar facts, but I can
assign them to no other cause than that I have
adduced.

I need scarcely observe that it is the object of
the merchant to ensure the perfect brilliancy of his
wine, and to preserve that brilliancy when attained. When wines in wood show any disposition to become flyery or cloudy, after having
been fined, the most prudent mode to adopt will
be to carefully rack such wine at once with a
bottling-cock, in order that the lees may be as
little disturbed as possible. I am aware that
many have an objection to racking wines, from an
idea that it weakens them, but this is assuredly a
mistaken notion. I am convinced of the efficacy
of the plan I recommend, however delicate the
wine may be to which it is applied. Wines do
not lose an atom of their saccharine property
in being carefully and cleanly racked, while on
the other hand we rid them, by that operation, of
whatever is opposed to their vinous perfection.
I have achieved far greater advantages by atten-
tiveness in racking and applying a moderate dose
of finings, than I have ever derived from any other
mode of treatment. It is much the practice with
the British merchant and cooper to administer a
top fining, when wines are found somewhat stub-

born, and this sometimes repeated two or three
times over. To say the least of such a system, it
is decidedly injudicious, and in nineteen instances
out of twenty the wine becomes in a greater or
less degree either flyery, cloudy, or foul in
bottle.

We perceive occasionally, in wines in bottle,
flyers assuming two different appearances; sometimes they may be seen floating in the form of a
flaky substance, yet the wine will show bright
with that exception; and at other times they
appear as exceedingly small dark crystal-like
particles; and on the bottle being shaken, the
wine immediately becomes foul. In other instances, a peculiarly fine sand-like sediment may
be observed at the side or in the punt of the
bottle. Some will persist that these deposits are
neither more nor less than crystallized tartar, and
that the Rhenish and French white wines are
most liable to be thus affected; others maintain
that the evil arises from some foreign admixture
introduced during the fermentation, or from the
blending of different varieties of wines previously
to the entire completion of the fermentation.
However, those who thus reason do so from mere
supposition; the probability is, that these defects
are attributable to the natural causes to which I
have just referred, and probably more often to the

want of proper treatment and the inefficacy of the fining.

I am aware that these accidents have been the subject of the keenest investigation, and many conjectures and arguments have been hazarded on their cause. The subject is, perhaps, scarcely susceptible of perfect explanation, but I conceive we cannot arrive at a more satisfactory conclusion than by referring these accidents generally to the causes I have assigned; that is, when the wines have been properly fined. I feel convinced that little can be advanced to impugn the accuracy of my remarks. Various have been the modes adopted in both the treatment and fining of wines, with the view of preventing these occurrences. No one will attempt to deny that it is essential before bottling to separate the wine from any abundance of lee; this, of course, can only be effected by efficient fining and racking, which should be performed in the most careful manner, so as to prevent any agitation in the lees, in order that we may not disturb that objectionable matter from which we desire to rid the wine. Hence, at the time of bottling, there will be but little sediment to disturb, and we thus avoid, as much as possible, the ascendancy of flyers, or other deposited matter. These are operations most beneficial, and indispensably necessary for per-

fecting the permanent brilliancy and condition of
wines.

The finest classes of Hocks, White Burgundy,
Moselle, Hermitage, Amontillado, Sherry, and
the pure Sercial Madeira, are, indisputably, the
choicest of white wines, yet we must admit, that
they are liable to these accidents, as well as wines
of inferior quality, though less frequently and in a
much less degree, when proper attention and appropriate finings have been used. I have in the
preceding remarks, I conceive, clearly shown
the cause of the tendency in the pure and perfect
wine, and of the ordinary or inferior wines, to deposit early in wood that tartarous quality, which
no one will deny to exist, in some degree, in all
wines, until they have attained their perfect state
of maturity. Experience teaches us that the freer
the fruit is from any tartarous impurity, the finer
will be the product. Thus it is, from this natural
cause, that the perfect wines more readily and
freely deposit those qualities necessarily present
in perfecting the fermentation. Hence wine gradually ameliorates until it has attained its maturity, and for the perfection of its brilliancy a simple
fining only is needed. It is not so with the
ordinary and inferior class of wines; they retain,
in suspension, more or less, some particles of the

impure qualities of the grape; hence the imperfection of this character of wine.

The preceding remarks, I hope, will serve in some measure to assist the inexperienced merchant and cooper in the treatment best adapted to the different qualities of wine, and enable them prevent, in a great degree, their wines from becoming flyery, cloudy, and foul in bottle.

I have often heard many remark, on discovering these imperfections, that the finings were properly prepared and applied, and that the wine was bottled perfectly bright; that every care was bestowed upon it, and they could not account for the change in bottle. I grant, as I have already acknowledged, that it is a difficult problem to solve at all times satisfactorily, but I am greatly mistaken if, in these instances, we might not often, on close investigation, find something like neglect or want of efficient finings to be the cause. However, what ought to be done immediately on housing any delicate wine, by way of accelerating its brilliancy, and ensuring the maintenance of its condition, is to place the wine in as steady a temperature as possible, not under 50° Fahrenheit; and let the wine remain for a few days, until it feels the effect of the change of locality before we attempt to fine it. If it be a very delicate wine, be moderate in the quantity of finings used, a delicate wine invariably yielding more kindly to a moderate than an over dose of finings; while the subsided lee will generally be found more stable. I have very frequently, in the case of delicate wines, adopted the plan of boring the tap hole when the wine has been laid on the scantling, or previously to fining it, and driven in a cork, so as to save boring the cask in order to introduce the bottling-cock at the time of bottling the wine. This mode enables us to tap the cask with much less chance of disturbing the lee. Were this plan generally adopted, I am convinced, that it would often prevent the appearance of flyers, and the cloudiness often perceived in bottled wines: other rules are necessary to be observed to insure the quietness of lees. No damp rubbish, or wet sawdust, should be suffered to accumulate under the bulge of the cask, where the lees naturally rest; but whatever may tend to create or imbibe dampness, should be raked away, and if the earth under the cask be of a cold clayey nature, some mode should be adopted to subdue the influence of the cold upon the cask, in order that the lees may not become affected by it. These are precautions necessary to be observed in such cases, for, where the bulge of the cask rests near to a cold bottom, the lees very rarely become perfect, quiet, and compact, in which case the wine has not a fair chance of maintaining its brilliancy and condition. I know these are held as secondary matters with many, but when the wine is perceived to become foul in bottle, they will probably think it worth while to attend to the hints which I have thrown out on the subject.

It is admitted by men of the first practical experience, that about the time the vine puts forth its buds, there may, occasionally, be observed a sympathy between the wine stored in the cellar and the vine; that is, the lees of many sorts of wine become more or less affected at these periods. This is chiefly observed in wines not fully matured, or wines not above three years old. This sympathetic phenomenon occurs at the periods when the sap of the vine is rising, and is watched for by one experienced in the management of wines. The indications are palpable enough to a practised eye: one of the signs is, an almost invisible greyish vapour. Immediately that this is observed, the wine should be racked before it assumes a perfect dulness. At other times, abundance of flyers are discovered swimming in the wine. In this latter case, the wine rarely becomes suddenly foul. However, these are certain indications of disturbed lee, and therefore are sufficient grounds for racking, in order to separate the wine from the disturbed sediment, when it will immediately regain its brilliancy, and most probably become improved in condition.

In other instances the lees may only become so far disturbed by these sympathetic changes, as merely to throw up a few flyers, scarcely discernible, and which, after a few days, may perhaps disappear; but it may here be remarked, that in these cases we may reasonably infer the once-subsided lee to be in a fickle, unstable, and incompact state. Now, if the wines giving these indications be bottled, without having been first racked and cleared from the disturbing cause, the result will invariably be that the wine becomes, in a greater or less degree, flyery or foul in bottle. However, as regards these unfortunate occurrences, much depends on the natural disposition and quality of the wine. I have frequently known wines, after having been once fined, to retain their brilliancy for years; and I have known other wines, until they have become aged, to exhibit these strange sympathies every vintage, although they have had the best attention bestowed upon them; and I have often found it necessary to rack wines in spring and autumn, in order to secure them from these contingencies.

It is astonishing, also, how these influences act on the aroma and flavour of some wines, if left to

E

themselves during the disturbed state of lees.
The question, therefore, is, what plan of treatment
promises most success, with reference to the permanent condition and brilliancy of wines so
affected ?

To this point I shall now address myself.

In the first place, it is necessary that the cause
of the disturbance of the lee, after its supposed
subsidence in wines, should be well considered.
Now we know these accidents are often productive
of great inconvenience, and when they occur
to wines in bottle are of serious consequence.
When we have good reasons for suspecting that
the deposited lee has become disturbed, from whatever cause, the proper course to pursue will be to
rack the wine so affected.   By this operation we
are enabled to separate the wine from the further
contamination of the disturbed lees, and other objectionable matter.

The British merchants and coopers, however,
have commonly adopted, and still pursue, the system
of giving the wine, in these cases, what is termed
a top fining, which, I contend, is most injudicious,
when the maintenance of brilliancy of the wine in
bottle is the object.   In the first place, we cannot
properly administer the fining without disturbing
the whole body of subsided lees, and bringing
back into suspension the sedimental matter, thus

strengthening the already excited fermentative principle which causes the disturbance. We may force back the substances affected, but we do not rid the wine from their influence. It is necessary to bear in mind, in these instances, that these changes are attributable to some active instigator of the fermentative principle present in the lees. One fact favourable to this conclusion may, at all events, be adduced, which is, that when wines to which these accidents occur are left to themselves, in nineteen instances out of twenty, they revert to almost their original foul condition. I do not assert that we cannot in these instances reproduce the brilliancy of the wine with the ordinary finings, without recourse to racking; what I assert is, that the system affords little or no security for the future condition and permanent brilliancy of the wine in wood, and especially in bottle.

The plan I recommend is, I am satisfied, the most advisable: it is to carefully rack the wine from the lees, which, with the assistance of suitable finings, insures the maintenance of its condition and brilliancy, both in wood and bottle.

I have dwelt at some length on the qualities of which it is essentially necessary a fining should consist; and I have endeavoured to make apparent the necessity of variation in the application of finings, corresponding with the different qualities of wines.   During my experience, of forty years, in the practical management of wines, I have witnessed many fatal results, from these important operations being performed by persons ignorant of their business ; as also from the application of unsuitable finings.   I shall, therefore, in dismissing this subject, prescribe a few rules applicable to different descriptions of wines generally found in the merchants' cellar, for the guidance of those who may be desirous of improvement, and feel disposed to adopt a system, the efficiency of which practice will abundantly demonstrate.

ON THE APPLICATION OF FININGS.

First, put the finings into a clean wooden can, or some other vessel that is perfectly clean and convenient for mixing the finings, add about two quarts of the wine to the finings, and whisk it gently up for a minute or two ; then add three or four quarts more of the wine, and mix the whole together with either the whisk or rousing stick, but do not agitate the finings so as to cause much froth. Now, if the following plan be adopted in pouring the finings into the cask, in two portions (particularly for a pipe or butt of wine), instead of pouring the whole in at one time, the finings will be more equally distributed over the surface of the wine ; for, with a little expertness in the use of the rousing stick, we are enabled to catch the finings before they have sunk too deep in the wine. To effect this perfectly, we ought to endeavour, whilst rousing the wine, to throw the fining to each head of the cask, and not continue throughout the operation to rummage all one way. Many cellarmen persist in rummaging the wine round one way only, and fancy it is the most systematic mode. However, I object to that plan ; maintaining that it is necessary for perfectly uniting and spreading the fining over the surface of the wine, to work the rousing stick different ways, in the commencement of the operation, moving it from head to head, as well as round. There is no occasion to particularly agitate the wine, but only to take full and efficient strokes with your rousing stick, so as to send the fining the greatest possible distance ; and, lastly, before withdrawing the rousing stick, to rouse the wine round one way by ten or twelve steady strokes, in order, after the finings having been perfectly united, to draw the precipitating matter to the centre, so that the deposit may be made as much in the bellying part of the cask as possible. A rousing stick ought

not to be more than three feet long for the purpose
of rousing in the finings of a pipe or butt of wine,
and two feet and a half for hogsheads, aums, &c.

The great object, as I have just remarked, in
rousing the finings into wines, is to unite and
spread them so as to form, as it were, a sheet upon
the whole surface of the wine, that the fining may
have the desired effect on all the particles floating
and suspended in it.

It has not unfrequently happened, as has
already been remarked, when this operation has
been performed in a slovenly manner, and the
finings have not been properly united, particularly
when wine is in a rather unfavourable temperature, that flyers are observed to linger in the wine ;
the same remark applies also to bottling wines
thus carelessly fined, which have appeared bright
from the fosset.   We may often perceive a few
bottles to run flyery ; and, at intervals, the wine
will run brighter at one time than at another : it
may happen that a bottle or two may appear a little
cloudy, then again the wine may run bright, or,
probably, become so foul as to render it prudent
to stay the further proceeding of bottling.   This
will generally happen near the end, or when the
cask is raised.   The result most annoying to the
merchant in these occurrences, is the whole bulk

of the wine becoming flyery or foul in bottle; but,
even if the evil should be only partial, the discovery at the consumer's table is anything but desirable, as detracting from that satisfaction which
the merchant is desirous at all times to give; consequently it behoves the cellarman or manager of
any stock of wines, to pay the strictest attention
to the judicious application of his finings.

The fact of which the merchant or cellarman
has first to satisfy himself, previous to the application of a fining, is the intrinsic purity of the wine.
He then only needs a fining prepared in the most
simple yet appropriate way, to perfect the brilliancy of the wine, and to counteract its liability
to the accidents already alluded to; while he
must bear in mind that occasions may arise to render it necessary to once rack and refine such wine.
Now, the first and principal requisite in a white
wine fining, is the purity of the isinglas; the
next is the fitness of the ingredient to dissolve it.
I know no mode of dissolving isinglas, combining
wholesomeness and efficacy, to surpass the following. I have tested its value in some hundred tuns
of different white wines. It consists in first mixing a portion of some dry wine with an equal portion of Rhenish stum, and then dissolving the
isinglas in it, by placing the vessel containing the
ingredients in some warm place,—say in a tem-

perature of seventy or eighty degrees of heat, allowing the fining two or three days for perfect dissolution.

TO MAKE FININGS FOR A PIPE OR BUTT OF WINE.

FROM RHENISH STUM ALONE.

For a pipe or butt of any delicate white wine, such as Amontillado, or any other fine pale sherry, Sercial Madeira, clean delicate Bucellas, &c., add to a quart of Rhenish stum half an ounce of the finest quality of picked isinglas; let it remain for two or three days to dissolve, during which time occasionally stir it up, as convenience offers, say two or three times in the day, after which it may be used, or reserved for future occasions. For a hogshead of wine we of course need but half these proportions, and for a quarter-cask one-fourth of the quantity designed for a butt; these proportions will be applicable to a hogshead of any kind of Rhenish or French white wines, to which a heavy fining is decidedly unsuitable, and which, above all other wines, need a fining of intrinsic purity.

It may here be proper to observe, that isinglas ought to be dissolved in an earthen vessel having a top, or otherwise secured by a covering of some sort, in order to preserve it from the influence of the air, dust, &c.; the common white jars with covers, which may be obtained at any of the earthenware shops, of various sizes, are well adapted for the purpose.

The ordinary full-bodied wines, as Sherry, Madeira, Lisbon, Teneriffes, Marsala, Capes, &c., require a larger portion of finings than those of a more delicate character, and for which the following increased proportions of isinglas and Rhenish stum will be found appropriate.

For a pipe or butt of full-bodied or ordinary wine, add to three pints of Rhenish stum three quarters of an ounce of isinglas, and dissolve it as already directed. Any quantity of finings that may be required is easily made by increasing the proportions of the Rhenish stum and isinglas. For instance; suppose you require a gallon of finings, you must then add the following proportions: one gallon of Rhenish stum to two ounces of isinglas; thus, it is easy to make whatever quantity of finings one's necessities require, by increasing accordingly the proportions of the Rhenish stum and isinglas.

It is evident that isinglas, from its nature, can gain after its dissolution no addition to its desirable properties; therefore it is obviously imprudent to make a larger quantity of finings at any one time than may be required for use within a reasonable period, say a month; by this precaution the merchant is secured against the liability of using any that may have become stale; such inadvertences it is very necessary to guard against.

TO DISCHARGE THE COLOUR OF WHITE WINES.

To discharge the colour of white wines so effectually as to render their ultimate brilliancy in bottle perfectly secure, is an object of much importance.

Sad errors have been committed from the systems pursued, and ingredients used for reducing the colour of wines, and very unfavourable results have occasionally ensued from the practice of such injudicious systems; I shall therefore adduce an uniform method, suitable to all kinds and qualities of wines.

The operation of reducing colour demands the cellarman's close attention, indeed, none of his operations in the cellar require a greater share of his skill and care, and without the observance of these he cannot perform his duty with credit to

himself, or to the interest of his employers.
There is a certain description of white wines,
which, from the nature of the grape, retains in the
skin more of the colouring matter than others, and
approximates in nature and quality to the tannin
matter found to exist in the skin of the grape,
from which port and other red wines are produced. These descriptions of white wines are generally coarser and more pungent than others; they
will often be found to improve when a portion of
the colour is extracted; their pleasantness of
flavour is much promoted, especially in the instance of wine that is somewhat coarse and high-
coloured; indeed, the general condition of these
wines may oftentimes be very materially improved, for this reason,—the degree of coarseness
and somewhat acrid quality which are frequently
found to exist in these wines, may be traced to the
tannin matter, or vegetable extract, with which
the skin of the grape becomes charged. The unfavourable quality is imbibed, in a greater or less
degree, according to the favourableness of the
season; thus, in wet and unfavourable seasons,
wines of such products are subject to the predominance of that quality which tends to im-
pede the amelioration of the wine, and robs it of
that agreeable flavour it might otherwise have
possessed. The decline of such wines is often

attributable, in some degree, to the presence of that extraneous quality when unchecked. We know that the ordinary finings, however appropriately prepared, have little or no effect on this peculiar quality, yet the extraction of colour is very simple, and the ingredients necessary for the purpose are perfectly unobjectionable.

We ought on all occasions, when about to subject any description of wine to a particular mode of treatment, to consider well the object we have in view, and then apply the means for effecting that object. Now, to do this, it is indispensably necessary thoroughly to have investigated the causes of the defects in wines, as well as the constituent qualities of the most pure and generous wines, before one can become sufficiently skilled in the management of them, as to be able, on tasting different qualities, to decide on the most judicious mode of treating them.

As regards the discharge of colour in different wines, Sherry will be found the most difficult wine to submit to that operation, and Madeira, Lisbon, Teneriffe, Marsala, and Capes, the most easy.

TO REDUCE A HIGH COLOURED WINE TO A LIGHT GOLD COLOUR.

Obtain, for a butt or pipe of white wine, three quarts of good milk, put it into a clean brass skillet, or some other appropriate vessel, place it over the fire until it just arrives at a boiling point, then pour it into a clean pan to cool, and when cool take off the scum which forms the greasy matter, and having so done, add to it half a pound of marine concrete; you will find by mixing them together that the milk will assume the appearance of thick cream; then add to it a gallon and a half or two gallons of the wine, keeping the whole well stirred during its addition; then pour it into the cask and rummage it well up for two or three minutes. When the wine is tolerably bright you may rack it; bag the bottoms if you think proper, and mix the bright wine with that racked, then fine it with the ordinary finings, bearing in mind that a stout full-bodied, or young wine, needs a larger quantity than a fully matured wine of a lighter character.

You will find, after a week or ten days' rest from this fining, that the wine will attain its perfect brilliancy; supposing it, however, to be a

F

coarse description of wine, and that you intend
to bottle it, then it would be prudent to rack it
a second time, in order to separate the wine, as
far as possible, from all objectionable matter that
has existed and become subsided; by pursuing
this plan you cannot fail to promote the development of all those desirable properties that
the wine possesses. It is from thus seasonably
racking this description of wines that we are
enabled to effect their general improvement, and
to ensure their brilliancy in bottle.

TO OBTAIN A PERFECTLY PALE WINE.

The portion of milk must depend on the colour
of the wine; it should also be remembered that
an old wine does not need so large a portion as a
young wine. Supposing it be desired to reduce
the colour of a high gold sherry to that of a pale
wine, and also that the wine be perfectly matured,
clean, and of a generous character, it will require
a gallon of milk and half a pound of concrete.
Now, if it should be convenient to first mix the
concrete and milk in two or three quarts of sweet
Lisbon, it will be found to have a very good
effect, inasmuch as with the concrete it tends in

a great measure, when mixed with the milk, to prevent its curding, and to counteract the coagulation which is a very desirable point. First, mix the concrete and milk together, then add the sweet wine, making the whole, together with the other wine, to about three gallons, keeping it well stirred up as you pour the wine to the milk, then pour half into the cask, and rummage the wine; after which pour in the remainder and rummage it again, by which means you catch the fining before it sinks too deep into the body of the wine. As soon as you find the wine tolerably bright, rack it carefully with a bottling-cock, after which fine it, and your own judgment will enable you to decide from the condition of the wine, whether or not it is needful to submit it to any farther operation of racking.

The principal things that we have to observe in reducing the colour of a wine, is the standard colour it possesses, its quality and state of maturity. If it is a pure and light character of wine, and the object is only to remove a portion of the colour, put two quarts of milk and a quarter of a pound of concrete to a pipe or butt of wine; and if it should be a young wine, we should need three quarts of milk and half a pound of concrete; if the object is to reduce the colour to a light straw colour, we must increase the quantity

of milk from three quarts to a gallon accordingly;
and in wines, particularly high-coloured, we require six quarts to attain our object, namely a
pale wine.

PREPARATION OF MILK.

I strongly recommend to those who have the
requisite convenience, the following plan, from
which it is impossible that the most delicate wine
can become in any degree injured, but, on the
contrary, I have known some instances of extra-
ordinary advantages accruing to the merchant
from the process. When you have obtained the
milk, put it into an earthen vessel that nicely contains the quantity required; then place the vessel
in a kettle nearly filled with cold water, put it on
the fire, and let the water boil gently until you
find the milk come to the same point, then remove
it and put it aside to cool. When cold you will
be enabled to abstract the entire greasy matter,
then add the concrete to it, and mix both well together. I have generally mixed a pint of milk
first with the concrete with the hand, and then
added the remainder by degrees. Thus we produce a preparation for reducing the colour of wines

that, for purity and efficiency, I am sure is not to be surpassed. After having completed this operation, I have generally adopted the plan, in cellars that have been free from vapours, of folding a clean piece of bung cloth three or four times thick, and tacking it over the bung-hole, instead of driving the shive in, and so have allowed it to remain until the wine was racked. But this plan must not be adopted with Rhenish or French wines; to all other wines it will be advantageous. It will be unnecessary for me here to give the proportions for a hogshead or quarter-cask, as they may be easily calculated from the quantity given to the pipe or butt. The object of mixing concrete with the milk is, that together they form a condensity which renders the preparation complete in its action, and it prevents the coagulation of the milk when first administered to the wine, while it materially accelerates the separation of the peculiar matter intended to be extracted and deposited. It unites the subsident substances falling into deposit; it perfects the coalescence of the sediment, and counteracts the influence of the extracted substances on the milk when formed into lee, thereby obviating the dulness frequently perceived in wines when milk alone has been applied. In fact, milk and the marine concrete are admirably applicable for reducing the colour of

all kinds of white wines. The application of the
preparation is simple, its purity and wholesomeness indisputable, while it has not the slightest
ill flavour.

ON BLENDING WHITE WINES.

Many good reasons may be assigned for blending wines, but it will not be possible for me to
point out any uniform rule; the mode must be
regulated by the particular advantage desired in
the operation. The improvement of one quality
of wine may be contemplated by mixing with it
a certain portion of another, or it may be desired
to produce a certain quality of wine suited to some
particular purpose. However, in these operations,
when it is convenient, we ought, prior to mixing together different qualities of wines, to get them into
as bright and good condition as possible, in order
that the good quality of the one may have its full
influence in supplying the absence of it in the
other. We will say, for instance, that we have a
butt of sherry which is wanting in both body and
character, and that the object is to amend and
improve that wine; the first step is to apply an
appropriate fining, in order to rack it bright at

the time of its being blended; thus we get rid of
all that quality of lee which would be opposed to
the favourable influence of the richer wine.
Whenever it is intended to amend and improve
the character of an ordinary description of white
wine, the first object should be to get that wine
into as clean a condition as possible, so that the
richer wine may speedily contribute the benefit
desired.

The following method will generally be found
beneficial, when it is desired to amend or enrich
any ordinary white wines, or wines wanting richness. As I have just observed, the first thing to
be done is to get them as bright and as clean as it
is possible; we may then effect an improvement by
adding to a pipe or butt of such wine ten, twelve,
or fourteen gallons of sweet Lisbon. This mode
may be pursued with much advantage in all instances with an ordinary Sherry that wants body
and richness. Supposing we have a pipe or butt
of wine that is somewhat worn, and become a
little harsh, and which we are desirous to improve,
in order to bring that wine into use. Then, in
fining that wine, give it one pound of the concrete and rack it, after allowing it to rest a week
or so for the subsidence of lee; then add such a
portion of sweet Lisbon as may be deemed necessary to produce the degree of richness desired,

after which use a moderate fining. The adoption of this mode cannot fail in every instance of producing the best results in thin and worn wines.

TO REMEDY THE ACCIDENTAL MALADIES IN WINES.

The accidental maladies in wines generally arise from the cask, or from negligence in respect of the vessels made use of in racking. But whatever be the cause, the remedy is usually a troublesome matter. A woody taste is very difficult oftentimes to get rid of, and a musty one is much more so. Innumerable recipes are given for the cure of these evils, as well known to the reader, I presume, as to myself; but I question if the best have been found effectual in practice. I have occasionally succeeded in remedying these defects by pursuing the following method:—For a butt or pipe of white wine, get your baker to well bake one pound of flour; put it into an earthen dish, so that it may lie about an inch thick in it; provide two quarts of milk, and when the flour is baked, mix it completely with the milk, so as to form one perfect consistence; then add half a pound of marine concrete: mix

the whole well together and fine the wine with it.
For a hogshead or quarter cask, you have only to
reduce the proportions accordingly. When the
wine is bright, rack it and fine it with the ordinary finings. Now this system is perfectly
wholesome, and during my experience I have
found nothing more efficient. It may be proper
to observe, that, in dealing with these maladies, it
is necessary to discharge a portion of the colour;
indeed it is scarcely possible to effect much good
without doing so; for this purpose we use the
milk, the flour and concrete act as absorbents,
the wine losing a portion of its colour at the same
instant that it gets rid of the defect.

In red wines we have greater difficulty, for this
reason—we cannot prudently reduce the colour;
and without removing that we cannot well
remedy the defect. However, the mode to be
pursued is, to use a pound and a half of flour, and
half a pound of concrete to a pipe of port or other
red wine, and then fine the wine with eight or ten
eggs. If this has not the desired effect, apply a
second dose, by using a pound of flour and a quarter of a pound of concrete, and then again fine the
wine with the same quantity of the whites of eggs,
and rack the wine when bright.

GENERAL REMARKS.

I am aware that there are some who make little or no distinction in the treatment of the different kinds of white wines. Wines widely differing from each other in quality, the products of different soils and climates, of different ages, and of different states of maturity, one and all have the same attention paid to them,—the mode of treatment and proportion of finings adapted for the one are deemed equally applicable to the others. But it is a rough and very injudicious practice, and often operates unfavourably. I have known many suffer for their obstinacy, although the majority of merchants well know that it is indispensable to the healthiness of many qualities of wine, that they should each have that attention which its particular nature requires. There are many great errors committed in the application of finings, not unfrequently arising from prejudices and want of experience, and I will venture to assert, that even in one sort and shipment of wines, necessities exist for variation of treatment and finings. I have, in the course of my remarks, dwelt at some length on this subject, and, I hope, sufficiently to enable most persons to form a just idea of the principle upon which it is permanently advantageous to act.

Some persons, with a view to hasten the brilliancy of white wines, in cases of pressing necessity, apply a heavy fining, as it is termed, that is, they employ a larger quantity of finings than is usual, in order, as they imagine, speedily to attain the desired object; but the practice is generally found to be deceptive, and it very frequently brings on a flatness in the wine from which it takes some time to recover, especially if it should be a wine of a light character. Now, in the event of any urgent demand to expedite the brightness of any white wine, in order that you may bottle a portion of it, say, for instance, in three or four days, the following method will be found successful.

For a pipe or butt of wine, dissolve half a pound of white candy in a pint of Rhenish stum, first breaking the candy as small as possible, which can be done with the face of the adze; then put it with the Rhenish stum* into a can or some other vessel which will admit of its being stirred about while it is dissolving, which it will do in about four or five hours. Stir it about at intervals with your rousing stick, so as to complete the dissolution; this done, add to it three

* The Rhenish stum is prepared by W. H. Rolfe and Co., Wine Fining Makers, No. 3, Great Tower Street, London.

pints of finings, and mix both up with a gallon of sweet Lisbon, or other sweet wine if convenient. You may then add to it about a gallon of the wine you intend fining, stir the whole together and proceed to fine the wine. When completed, leave the shive loose, in order to allow sufficient vent.

In cases of emergency I have often, from the adoption of this mode, succeeded in perfecting the brilliancy of wines in the time just specified. Nevertheless, I am no advocate for the system, unless it be in some pressing occasion, for reasons sufficiently obvious to every person familiar with the treatment of wines; all wines necessarily requiring a longer time for the gradual subsidence of the lees.

IN FINING RHENISH AND FRENCH WHITE WINES.

I have frequently derived advantage, when fining the Rhenish and French white wines, by first mixing the finings with a bottle of sweet wine, such as Lunelle and Frontignac, letting it rest an hour or two before I fined the wine. The plan may seem frivolous to some, but those who have not made the trial, will find it worthy of their notice. I have often perfected the brilliancy of a hogshead of wine by this very simple method, after it had been variously operated upon with finings without the desired effect; and the wines will generally show greater brilliancy after this operation, and rarely become flyery or foul in bottle. When it is not convenient to obtain a bottle of sweet French wine, a bottle of good clean sweet Lisbon can do no harm; indeed, in some instances, a much larger portion would be serviceable for the nutrition of many of these wines.

If the mode of treatment and the finings I prescribe be adopted, they will, I am convinced, wholly supersede the use of those doubtful ingredients of which I have disputed the applicability. Now, with respect to such wine as has become perfectly acid, it would be presumptuous to suppose that they are to be made marketable by the aid of any fining whatever; in fact, such an achievement I am sure is not desired by the merchants; it is impossible to restore such degenerated wines to a wholesome condition. I am not ignorant of the means adopted to correct, in a great degree, such degenerated wines; nevertheless, I must think those who adopt and carry the system into practice ought to drink the wine themselves. What I contend for is, the expediency of averting

G

such maladies, by applying at a seasonable period, a wholesome and efficient fining, adapted to the necessities of any ordinary or affected wine, whereby we may correct the threatened evil. I maintain that if complete control is not attainable, by skilful treatment and appropriate finings, over the defects frequently found to exist in the ordinary and inferior class of wines, much more may be done to remedy such defects than has hitherto been achieved, that the general amelioration of such wines may be greatly promoted by timely accelerating and perfecting the subsidence of the extraneous matter suspended in them.

Professor Liebeg and others insist that in the grapes poor in sugar there remains, according to circumstances, after the completion of the process of fermentation, a portion of nitrogenous constituents, retaining the same properties which were possessed by the grape previous to the fermentation. These assertions must, I presume, tend to confirm the truth of my observations with regard to the treatment of the ordinary and inferior classes of wines, and to show also the expediency of a fining specifically applicable for divesting such wines, in some degree, of their obnoxious qualities. Now for this purpose the *Concret Marin** is specifically designed. The principle is

* *Smeed's Concret Marin* bears the name on the seal,

acknowledged by merchants generally to be perfectly clear, and yet, obvious as it is, there are some who cannot understand its value. I feel assured of its universal adaptation to the ordinary wines, to the defects of which it will be found advantageously applicable.

RACKING.

In racking wine intended to be bottled, the first object is to procure a fresh cask, emptied of as good a wine as possible; then we ought to be particular in the cleanliness of the cans or vessels made use of in the operation; the shive should be loosened in order to allow the wine full and efficient vent while it is running off; and before we commence racking, we ought to bore a vent-hole in the bung stave of the empty cask, either before or behind the funnel, so that the confined air in the empty cask may escape as we pour in the wine. By this means we prevent the wine

encircled in that of W. H. Rolfe and Co., 3, Great Tower-street, London, who are the principal agents. The observance of this on the seal of the packages may be very necessary.

becoming impregnated with the air previously
contained in the empty cask, which air we may
plainly hear escape from the vent-hole as the cask
fills, and we hereby also prevent any bubbling
over from the funnel, thus precluding the possibility of the wine imbibing by contact any new ele-
ment, which is a very essential precaution to be
observed in racking operations, especially with delicate wines.   Moreover, the wine, after being
thus racked, immediately regains its quietude, and
as soon as the bottoms are bagged, if you think
proper to do so, the bright wine from the bag
may be mixed with the finings, and the wine then
fined and shived up.   It must be borne in mind,
that after racking wines from the deposited lee,
a moderate fining only is required.   In the adoption of this mode we can depend on wines retaining their perfect condition and brilliancy, so
as to fit them for immediate bottling if desired, or
if left to rest, their amelioration will be promoted
by the operation.

Some imagine that wines lose both character
and body from the operation of racking; that is
altogether a mistaken notion.   Whenever there
is a necessity for racking wines, their pleasantness
of flavour, delicacy, &c. are invariably much
enhanced, provided the operation be properly
performed.   In fact, it is as I have before re-

marked on this subject, a sure mode of their pre-servation.

RHENISH AND FRENCH WINES.

The Rhenish and French wines require more attention and care on their coming into the hands of the merchant than any others. As their nature and delicacy will not admit of repeated rackings, or fortifying with brandy, whereby the nutrition of other wines is much more easily accomplished, a very pure and efficient fining in the first instance is an essential point. The chief care then required by these wines after being fined, consists in keeping the casks as free from ullage as possible, to prevent the atmospheric air resting on the surface of the wine, in order to secure it from that infection of mouldiness of which these wines are so susceptible, termed by some, the mother, by others the flower, &c. If, at the time of fining the wine, we take the precaution, provided the cask be not completely full, of burning a portion of a match by introducing it just within and round the shive hole, and immediately on withdrawing the match drive in the shive, it will, in ninety-nine cases out of a hundred, preserve the wine against the disease of mouldiness on its surface.

Many merchants dissolve the isinglas with Hock, and other Rhenish wines, when anxious to procure a very pure fining on a particular occasion, for some peculiarly delicate and probably expensive wine. It is well known to all conversant with the trade, that the Rhenish wines are more effectual than any other in dissolving isinglas; yet men of general experience agree, that however great the properties of those wines may be singly applied, in dissolving isinglas for finings, the result is not wholly to be depended upon for securing the absolute compactness and stability of lee. Now, a fining more pure it is impossible to prepare; but the frequent occurrence of flyers in wines so fined sufficiently shows the deficiency of the needful basis in the preparation to complete the stability of the matter deposited; it is therefore very evident that we need an addition of some ingredient, as the basis of the fining, to render it complete; it is of great importance to those who make their own finings to bear this in mind; the method of preparation must be based upon this principle to render the fining permanently effective.

DIFFERENCE OF TREATMENT NECESSARY
FOR WINES.

I have before observed that different wines require different treatment, as they differ from one another in their natural qualities. For instance, if you house a butt of very fine clean delicate Sherry, you need only apply to such a wine an ordinary fining, and then proceed in the further treatment of it as has been already recommended. But, on the other hand, allowing that you take into stock a wine of ordinary character, and that some slight defect, one, probably, of the many I have alluded to, is found to exist in it, it becomes prudent to resort to the marine concrete. When there is very little defect, a small portion only of the marine concrete is required, say half or three quarters of a pound to a pipe or butt of wine, as may be judged necessary. This ought to be well mixed up in five or six quarts of the wine, then poured into the cask, and well rummaged up with a rousing stick; the ordinary finings may then be used without the least regard whatever to the concrete. When the wine is bright, rack it, and fine it again with about two-thirds of the ordinary finings you previously used. Now, supposing that after this operation the wine,

on attaining its brilliancy, is not quite so clean as
was expected, or not to your perfect satisfaction :
then do not hesitate to rack it again, and again
reduce the quantity of ordinary finings ; by these
means, and only by these means, can you ever
effect a permanent improvement in the ordinary or
inferior class of wines.

As regards the generality of ordinary wines, we
know the variety of quality to be very great;
the cause of which, whether natural or incidental,
I have already commented upon, and I hope
sufficiently, to enable both the merchant and cellarman to discern and judge of the necessity for
variation in finings and treatment, and to pursue
a course adapted to the wants of whatever description of wine may come into their hands.
However, in order to render this particular duty
in the cellar more clear to those who are wanting
in experience, we will be supposed to have housed
a butt or pipe or two of ordinary wine, and that
we previously knew their precise quality, or we
find it out when tasting them in the cellar, which
ought always to be done before they are fined.
Now, we will allow the first to be a good clean
ordinary wine and perfectly matured; satisfied of
this, we have only to administer an ordinary
fining.   But the second butt or pipe we find
rather inferior; there is a coarseness and some-

thing objectionable in flavour hanging about it. Then, if it be a butt, use a pound of concrete, if a pipe, three quarters of a pound, and afterwards fine it with the ordinary finings in the manner repeatedly adverted to. Now bear in mind, that when the concrete is used, the wine generally falls bright very soon, therefore you may always calculate that it will be in order for racking in a week after such a fining. Thus you have complete control over the brilliancy and condition of the wine, after having once racked it from the original lees. After the wine is racked and fined, and again bright, which will be sure to be the result in a few days, your own judgment will best guide you, whether or not it is necessary to rack the wine a second time; if you have so far effected an improvement as to be satisfied with the wine, then there will be no need of further operations. If, however, it should not be so clean or satisfactory as you anticipated, and there is still something objectionable about it, it becomes advisable to rack it a second time, and give it a lighter fining than you used in the last operation.

Again, you may have a butt or a pipe of wine which may be both harsh and coarse, yet, perhaps, possessing tolerable body, and it may also happen that you have a wine harsh without coarseness, and with few other defects to complain of. Now,

in either of these cases, you ought invariably to
use from a pound to a pound and a half of concrete to a butt, and a pound or a pound and a
quarter to a pipe of wine, bearing in mind that it
will, at all times, be necessary to rack this description of wines twice at least, because, whether
you intend to bottle them or to blend them, the
cleaner you get them the better they become
qualified for the purpose. And here it may be
remarked, that, in nine instances out of ten, the
ordinary wines have been blended, brought into
use, and bottled, before they have been properly
cleaned. Now it must be very obvious that all
wines possessing any defect require to be submitted to a prudent mode of treatment, in order
to divest them of the objectionable quality present.
In these instances, we are enabled, by the addition of the concrete, to effect the subsidence of all
extraneous substances so present and suspended;
the same being secured in deposit. We are also
enabled by racking the wine, and repeating the
operation of racking as necessity requires, to entirely divest the wine of all obnoxious particles,
thus developing its desirable qualities. Madeira
of ordinary quality, Teneriffe, and, indeed, most
of the Azores, the Italian and Sicilian wines, are
more susceptible of harshness than Sherries and
the generality of Spanish and Portuguese wines.

Many of these wines may be found in the bonded cellars in a complete state of degeneracy. Now if, at the time these wines were first housed, or at a reasonable period afterwards, a pound of the concrete had been used to a pipe, with or without the assistance of any other fining, it would have been of the greatest benefit to them. That tartarous quality, so detrimental to the generous property of these wines, would become so far neutralized as to admit of their improvement and amelioration, instead of their becoming harsh and falling into decline, particularly if racked when bright from the subsidence of the lee; this affords the means, after having been fined with the concrete, of totally freeing the wine from the deteriorative quality to which the decay of these wines may be attributed. I am satisfied that it would abundantly repay the owner of this description of wines, if he were to adopt this system. If he do so, and deem it prudent to fortify the wine with a gallon of brandy, or any portion he thinks proper, it will secure the amelioration and preservation of the wine, and enable the safe shipment of it to any part of the world. The same rule of treatment is also applicable to Cape wines. The influence of the concrete is equally successful in divesting these wines of their objectionable flavour, and in effecting their general improvement.

OF PORT WINES.

The treatment is very simple with pure and good ports, which are invariably fined in this country with the whites of eggs, as are also most other red wines. The finings we know to be unobjectionable, provided the eggs are perfectly good. However, a very simple and advantageous addition is practicable, which renders the fining more efficient for establishing the perfect brilliancy and condition of ports and other red wines. When you break the eggs drop the whites into a pint of Rhenish stum; let them stand aside for an hour, then whisk them gently up, adding by degrees three or four quarts of the wine, and then proceed to fine it in your usual way. I have no doubt this mode may be thought unimportant by many, but simple as it may appear, it has the effect of giving a peculiar solidity to the fining, whereby its action is rendered more powerful, and as it undergoes no change in its properties by the effects of the peculiar astringent qualities of ports, when brought to operate upon, and whilst in the act of combining with the lees, it insures, in the most complete manner, the permanent brilliancy of the wine.

Port wines that have become worn, and probably wanting in character and colour as well as body, require to be blended or brought up by the addition of more youthful wine; you need, in that case, such a quantity of young and rich wine as will bring up the one and ameliorate the other. By these means, when an old wine is perfectly clean and sound, you may often effect an improvement by properly blending with it a younger wine. It will be difficult here to point out any regular method for these performances; it must depend much upon the judgment of the holder, or person who has the management of them, and on the quality of the wines to be blended, as well as on the character of wine which it is your object to make up.

But, as regards the inferior quality of port wines, you must pursue a different course. If you happen to have a pipe of port that is either coarse, harsh, or unpleasant in its flavour, it becomes prudent to eradicate such defects as far as possible before you blend or make any use of such a wine. Now, to remedy these defects, you cannot possibly adopt any better mode than that of using the marine concrete, as recommended for white wines.

A coarse or harsh pipe of port will require a pound and a half of concrete; mix the concrete with about two gallons of the wine, and stir the

whole well together before you pour it into the
cask ; then rummage it well about with your
rousing stick, and afterwards you may fine the
wine with the whites of fourteen or fifteen eggs,
as you would have done had you not used the
concrete. Or if it be convenient, it will be as
well to fine the wine with eggs the day after using
the concrete. For a hogshead or quarter cask,
you will have of course to reduce the proportions
accordingly. You may find the wine linger for
a week or ten days in a dullish state, after being
thus treated ; but soon after it is racked you will
discover a material improvement. Another important advantage has been proved to be derivable
from this system of treatment, namely, that the
crust of port wines thus treated generally adheres
firmly to the bottle. This arises from the influence of the concrete in the neutralization of the
peculiar tartarous qualities of these wines, which
are well known to differ from most other description of wines. It may happen that we want to
enrich a pipe of port, and find it inconvenient
to procure the quantity of richer port needful to
the purpose ; in that case we can adopt the following method, which is to use eight or ten gallons
of rich mountain, or half that quantity of Tent,
either at the time you use the concrete, or after
the wine has been racked from the influence of

that fining, as you may think proper. In ordinary ports it will tend to the attainment of your object.

With respect to the generality of other red wines, with the exception of Rhenish and French, the system of treatment varies so little, that it would be uselessly lengthening my remarks to dwell on them.

RHENISH AND FRENCH RED WINES.

Of all red wines produced, there are none that require so much care and skill as the first rate Burgundys, Hermitage, and Clarets. These wines, from their great delicacy and nicety of flavour, will scarcely admit of the least portion of brandy or any other admixture, without immediately showing the impregnation and degree of contagion. Therefore those who may have the care and management of these wines will, it is presumed, see the necessity of administering the cleanest and most efficient fining it is possible to procure, and at the time of fining the wines to be careful not to expose them to the atmospheric influence, by allowing the shive to remain out any longer than is really necessary during any process

to which they may be submitted. The fining
suitable to a hogshead of these wines is particularly simple, and from the abundant proofs I have
experienced of its efficacy, I recommend its universal adoption. It consists of the whites of six
or seven newly laid eggs added to a pint of Rhenish
stum.

When you break the eggs to separate the whites,
drop them into a bottle, or some vessel containing
a pint of Rhenish stum, and put it aside for an
hour or so, then if convenient fine the wine. I
have generally used a magnum to shake the
finings in, or a two or three quart jug. Never
whisk up the finings in a wood can for these delicate wines; I have known many bad results to
arise from that practice. When you fine these
wines, either shake up the eggs briskly with the
Rhenish stum in a magnum, or beat them up
gently with it with the whisk in a jug.
When the eggs are incorporated, mix the whole
up with about two quarts of the wine. Be
careful, before you pour the finings into the cask,
that the rummaging stick is perfectly clean, and it
will be well to bear in mind that it is very essential
to first well incorporate the eggs with the Rhenish
stum before the wine is added to it; by so doing
we are better enabled to mix the eggs with the
wine without causing over much froth, which is

necessary to be avoided in fining these wines. As soon as the wine is fined, we ought invariably to burn a small portion of sulphurated match within the shive-hole, or fold a bit of thick paper dipped in a little brandy, and burn it as far within the shive-hole as possible; then drive in the shive immediately the flame is exhausted; it will then be prudent to wet a little plaster of Paris, or some other cement, and cement the shive-hole over to prevent the possibility of ingress of air. If the mode I here recommend be strictly adhered to, it will be found effectual in completing the brilliancy of these wines, and serve as a preventive to the maladies to which they are at present exposed.

The method generally resorted to by the fabricator after the completion of fermentation, to check the exciters of harshness and acescency with a view to the preservation of wine, is the system of sulphuration. It is well known that this is effected by burning a piece of sulphur, or a sulphurated match, adapted to the purpose, in the cask destined to receive the wine racked. The vaporous influence of the sulphurous property diffused through the wine corrects, to an extent, the detrimental quality present, and withdraws all the oxygen the wine may have absorbed from the atmosphere. The applicability and necessity of this principle have recently been most accurately described, and its efficacy as fully demonstrated by Professor Liebeg in his lectures on vinous fermentation given at the university of Giessen. He contends, as indeed do all the great scientific men of the present day, that if we possess any means practically applicable for perfectly separating all those substances which are the cause of harshness and the acescent quality (either during or soon after the completion of fermentation), we should be able to preserve wine in a state of greater salubriousness, and for a much longer period than has been generally effected.

It may be easily conceived, as is acknowledged by men of the greatest practice, that an absolutely perfect separation of all objectionable substances (which are rarely entirely absent in the fruit undergoing fermentation) is attained only in a few favourable instances, "when the exceeding favourable circumstances occur tending to augment these desired attainments." The wine we know thus obtained is invariably superior in quality to that which is produced from grapes that may in some slight degree be less favourably matured, or that have imbibed, to a certain extent, some quality foreign to the pure vinous properties. Thus it becomes indispensably necessary for the fabricator, factor, or merchant, to exercise his best means and skill to decompose and extract to the utmost the foreign matter so present.

Now, before I conclude, I beg to invite the merchant's attention to this subject, which I conceive to be the most important to him. We know that wine progresses in maturity, and every other desirable quality proportionably to its intrinsic purity; therefore it must be very evident to a discerning mind, that to allow any separable substance to remain lingeringly suspended in wines is highly imprudent. If experimental art has discovered a simple and wholesome remedy applicable to this object, the propriety of its adoption is manifest, since it must prove invaluable whenever any degree of coarseness, unpleasantness of flavour, or harshness is perceptible in wines, arising from the causes referred to in my preceding remarks. A specific fining is indispensably requisite for the neutralization and abstraction of the exciting qualities that prevent the development of the vinous property. The fining I have recommended to be used in these instances, namely, the marine concrete, is one incomparably the most perfect known in practice; the exceedingly favourable influence which the concrete exercises upon the purification of wines can only be appreciated by those who have adopted it.

With respect to wine which is shipped in a youthful state, and before it has perfectly disengaged itself of all separable tartarous qualities, much may be done on these occasions, after their arrival in the bonded stores, to improve the general condition of such wines. If at the time of storing the wine away, a pound of concrete is used to a butt or a pipe, it will speedily avert and remedy the influence of any deteriorative matter which is commonly suspended in the wine at this period, and which by this process becomes combined with the perfect lee. By the adoption of this system, wines shortly attain the same maturity which, under ordinary circumstances, is the result of a long protracted period of storing. The same system is, of course, applicable equally to wines vatted; and when improvement is the object desired, the advantages afforded by this process of fining will prove to surpass any other mode of treatment.

It is upon this principle that the system of treatment must be based, to be permanently efficacious, whether adopted in wines in bond or in the merchant's cellar,—that is, with reference to any description of wine which we submit to a process of fining with a view to effect an improvement in its condition.

The method that has been employed by most

merchants has indisputably proceeded upon principles the very reverse of those advocated in this treatise. Much of the ordinary wine has been left too long unattended to, and when its degeneracy is suspected or perceived, the practice ordinarily adopted is to fortify it with brandy. But this method is not, by itself, in many instances, all-efficient. The fortifying certain kind of wines with brandy is unquestionably on some occasions very essential, singly applied; but I maintain that we cannot correct any ailment or defect to which wine is liable by the application of brandy alone. It is true, that we may, by its use, prevent and avert for a time certain incidental ailments; but we do not perfectly and permanently remedy them so as to promote the amelioration or preservation of wine. When improvement is sought for, first allow an appropriate fining to be employed to remove the cause of defect, or to perfect the condition of the wine; then, by the operation of racking, and the aid of such a portion of brandy as may be deemed necessary, we finally achieve every practicable advantage.

London:
Printed by STEWART and MURRAY,
Old Bailey.

January, 1845.

A

Catalogue

OF

INTERESTING WORKS,

IN THE PRESS OR RECENTLY PUBLISHED BY

SMITH, ELDER AND CO.,

65, CORNHILL, LONDON.

Preparing for Publication.

OBSERVATIONS IN THE SOUTHERN HEMISPHERE,

MADE DURING A RECENT RESIDENCE AT

THE CAPE OF GOOD HOPE.

By Sir John Herschel, Bart., F.R.S., &c.
To be Illustrated by numerous Plates.

JUST PUBLISHED,

In One Volume, post 8vo., cloth,

THE DUTIES OF JUDGE ADVOCATES.

Compiled from Her Majesty's and the Hon. East India Company's Military
Regulations, and from the works of various writers on Military Law.

By Captain R. M. Hughes,

12th regt. B. N. I., Deputy Judge Advocate General, Scinde Field Force.

JUST PUBLISHED,

In One Volume, post 8vo., price 10s. 6d., cloth, with a Portrait of Author,

CHRISTMAS FESTIVITIES: TALES, SKETCHES, AND CHARACTERS.

WITH BEAUTIES OF THE MODERN DRAMA,

IN FOUR SPECIMENS.

By John Poole, Esq.,
Author of " Paul Pry," &c. &c.

Now publishing in Quarterly Volumes,

THE WORKS OF G. P. R. JAMES, ESQ.

Price 8s. cloth,

Handsomely printed in medium 8vo, and Illustrated.

This new and attractive series of Mr. James's works commenced on the 1st of July with the "Gipsey," and was followed, on the 1st of October, by "Mary of Burgundy." The future volumes will be published Quarterly, each containing a complete work. The whole of this edition has been carefully revised by the author, and is got up in that superior style and agreeable size of type which render it fit for every age and for every library.

Vol. 3, containing the "Huguenot," a Tale of the French Protestants, will be published on the 1st January, 1845, and will contain, in addition to the usual Illustration, a new and highly-finished Portrait of the Author.

" Messrs. Smith, Elder & Co., of Cornhill, have just published the first volume of a New Edition of the works of this gentleman, which has the advantage of the latest revisions and corrections of the author. The writings of James are so well-known to the readers of fiction that it is unnecessary to call their attention to them, or to say anything as to their merits or defects, which previous criticism may have left unsaid. The present edition is well got up, there are few errata, the type is clear, sharp, and legible, and the size of the volumes convenient for the reader and appropriate for the shelves of a book-case. The frontispiece of the first volume illustrates that scene in the novel of the Gipsey, in which Lord Dewry is astounded in the prosecution of his villanous plot to destroy Pharhold, by the unexpected appearance of the person who passes under the name of Sir William Ryder. The book, as it is, will form a pleasing addition to the collections of readers of modern literature, of the class to which it belongs."

Times, August 17, 1844.

" We are glad to see our prognostication respecting the New Edition of Mr. James' Works, more than fulfilled by the rapid absorption of a very large first edition, and a second in the course of speedy disappearance. This is as it should be, with a writer whose vraisemblance is always so perfect; and even what he invents so like truth, that we can never fancy we are reading fiction, nor, indeed, are we, in the historical portions of his publications, — and these form the far greater division, — which are all drawn from diligent research, deep study, and elaborate comparison."

Literary Gazette, August 8, 1844.

" Mr. James is a pure and pleasing writer, and we are glad to see that his Works are now to be thrown into a handy, handsome, and accessible shape."

Scotsman, July 13, 1844.

"This is a most admirable edition of the Works of this popular author, convenient in size, and handsome in appearance. It, moreover, possesses the advantage of being revised and corrected by the author,—no small recommendations, since, the generality of Mr. James' Works being connected with history, a careful perusal of his productions, increases their value, and renders them a source of amusement, through the medium of instruction."

Atlas, October 20, 1844.

In post 8vo, price 10s. 6d., handsomely bound in a new kind of cloth, silver gilt, or 9s. boards,

IMAGINATION AND FANCY;

Or, SELECTIONS from the ENGLISH POETS, illustrative of those First Requisites of their Art: with Markings of the best Passages, Critical Notices of the Writers, and an Essay in Answer to the Question, "What is Poetry?"

By LEIGH HUNT.

"This volume is handsomely printed, and beautifully bound in a new style of exquisite delicacy and richness. To institute a comparison with the contents of the Annuals would be absurd, at any degree of distance,—there is no more relation between them than between a street lamp and a fixed star; but in external beauty 'Imagination and Fancy' equals any gift-books that have appeared; and it will form a more enduring memorial than any other volume that might be selected as a gift for the coming season."—SPECTATOR.

SECOND EDITION, REVISED by the EDITOR, with INTRODUCTORY COMMENTS,

In Two Vols., post 8vo., price 24s., cloth.

A NEW SPIRIT OF THE AGE.

Containing Critical Essays, and Biographical Sketches of Literary and other Eminent Characters of the Present Time.

EDITED BY R. H. HORNE, ESQ.
Author of "Orion," "Gregory the Seventh," &c. &c.

The volumes are illustrated with engravings on steel, from new and original portraits of DICKENS, TENNYSON, CARLYLE, WORDS-WORTH, TALFOURD, BROWNING, SOUTHWOOD SMITH, and MISS MARTINEAU.

"In the biographical sketches the Editor has carefully excluded all disagreeable personalities and all unwarrantable anecdotes. The criticisms are entirely upon abstract grounds. He may be often wrong, but it is with a clear conscience."—EDITOR'S PREFACE.

In 2 volumes post 8vo. illustrated with numerous Engravings on Steel, from new and original Portraits.

OUR ACTRESSES;
OR,

GLANCES AT STAGE FAVOURITES,
PAST AND PRESENT.

By Mrs. C. BARON WILSON.

Author of the "Life of the Duchess of St. Albans," "Memoirs of Monk Lewis," &c. &c.

"Handsome volumes adorned with several portraits, and the biographies are full of amusing anecdotes."—ATLAS.

"So attractive are the stage and its denizens that considerable amusement will be derived from the perusal of these pages."—LITERARY GAZETTE.

Just Published.

In 2 Volumes, Demy 8vo., with numerous Illustrations.   Price 34s., cloth.

THE MODERN HISTORY AND CONDITION OF EGYPT;

ITS CLIMATE, DISEASES, AND CAPABILITIES;

Exhibited in a Personal Narrative of Travels in that Country, with an Account of the Proceedings of Mahommed Ali Pascha, from 1801 to 1842, with Illustrations of Scripture History, the Fulfilment of Prophecy, and the Progress of Civilization in the East.

By W. HOLT YATES, M.D., &c. &c.

"He fulfils his historic vocation by an ample resumé of the more prominent incidents which have distinguished the fortunes of the Pascha, upon whose policy of general monopoly his strictures are severe enough, and acquits himself creditably from his spirited and highly coloured sketches of the abundant objects to which he draws attention."—MORNING HERALD.

In demy 12mo, Price 6s. cloth, pp. 340,

THE CONVICT SHIP.

A Narrative of the results of Scriptural Instruction and Moral Discipline, as these appeared on board the *Earl Grey*, during the voyage to Tasmania: with brief notices of individual Prisoners.

By COLIN ARROTT BROWNING, M.D.

Surgeon, Royal Navy; Author of "England's Exiles," &c.

In demy 8vo., Price 12s. cloth.

A DISSERTATION ON THE TRUE AGE OF THE WORLD.

AS ASCERTAINED FROM THE HOLY SCRIPTURES.

Containing a review of the Opinions of Ancient and Modern Chronologers, including Usher, Hales, Clinton, and Cuninghame, and a Chronological Table of the Principal Epochs and Events in Sacred and Profane History, from the Creation to the present Time.

By PROFESSOR WALLACE.

"It is learned and laborious."—BRITANNIA.

Sixth Edition, in 3 vols. 8vo. beautifully illustrated, Price 7s. 6d. each, in a handsome and uniform cloth binding, or 10s. 6d. morocco.

PICTURES OF PRIVATE LIFE;

By MRS. ELLIS,

Author of "The Women of England," &c. &c.

Contents: Vol. I. "Observations on Fictitious Narrative," "The Hall and the Cottage," "Ellen Eskdale," "The Curate's Widow," and "Marriage as it May Be."

   ,,   Vol. II. "Misanthropy," and "The Pains of Pleasing."

   ,,   Vol. III. "Pretension; or, the Fallacies of Female Education."

Each Volume is complete in itself, and may be purchased separately.

Just Published.

Post 8vo., Price 7s. 6d. boards.

EXPERIMENTAL RESEARCHES, CHEMICAL AND AGRICULTURAL.

Part I. contains, Carbon a Compound Body made by Plants, in quantities varying with the circumstances under which they are placed. Part II. Decomposition of Carbon during the Putrefactive Fermentation.

By ROBERT RIGG, F.R.S.

SECOND EDITION, Price 12s. cloth.

MODERN PAINTERS:

Their Superiority in the ART of LANDSCAPE PAINTING to all the Ancient Masters, proved by examples of the True, the Beautiful, and the Intellectual, from the Works of Modern Artists, especially from those of J. M. Turner, Esq., R.A.

By a GRADUATE of OXFORD.

"This is the production of a highly gifted mind, one who has evidently bestowed time and labour to obtain a practical knowledge of the fine arts, and who writes eloquently, feelingly, and fearlessly."—POLYTECHNIC REVIEW.

"It has seldom been our lot to take up a work more elaborately conceived and written than this beautiful and elaborate essay."—ATLAS.

In 2 Vols., Demy 8vo., Price 32s. cloth.

With a Large Map by Arrowsmith, and Illustrated with Plates.

NOTES AND OBSERVATIONS ON

THE IONIAN ISLANDS AND MALTA,

WITH SOME REMARKS ON

CONSTANTINOPLE AND TURKEY;

And on the system of Quarantine, as at present conducted.

By JOHN DAVY, M.D., F.R.SS. L. & E.
Inspector-General of Army Hospitals, L.R.

"Dr. Davy's work deserves to be bought as well as perused, so carefully, completely and expensively has it been got up. We hope that the consciousness of having discharged such an important duty will not be the only result of his long labour, but that the work will prove as remunerative as it ought to be."—WESTMINSTER REVIEW.

"There probably is not another work in our language in which so ample and substantially useful an account is given of the Ionian Islands as is here to be found. There can be little doubt that to these volumes will be assigned an honourable place amongst the recognized master-works of the class to which they belong."—MORNING HERALD.

Just Published.

Second edition, 1 vol. post 8vo., with an entirely New Map, Price 12s. cloth.

HAND-BOOK FOR INDIA AND EGYPT ;

Comprising Travels from Calcutta, through India, to the Himalaya Mountains, and a Voyage down the Sutledge and Indus Rivers ; a Visit to the City of Hyderabad, in Scinde ; and the Journey to England by the Red Sea and Mediterranean : with Descriptions of the Three Presidencies of India ; and the fullest details for parties proceeding to any part of India, either by the Overland Route, or by the way of the Cape of Good Hope.

By GEORGE PARBURY, Esq., M.R.A.S.

. The press, both of Great Britain and India, have combined in eulogizing the value of this work, but it may only here be needful to quote the following remarks from the editorial columns of the *Standard* of the 10th April, 1843 : " We have elsewhere copied from Mr. Parbury's Hand-Book to India and Egypt, an interesting account of the City of Hyderabad. Let us, in acknowledgment of the means afforded to us to inform and gratify our readers, say of Mr. Parbury's work, as we may with truth, that it is the best Topographical Guide to the countries to which it refers we have ever seen, a most interesting book, independently of its topographical utility, and an almost indispensable key to the late transactions in Central Asia."

Price 2s. 6d. bound in cloth.

CROSBY PLACE,

Described in a Lecture on its Antiquities and Reminiscences delivered in the Great Hall on the evening of Friday, August 5th, 1842.

By the Rev. CHARLES MACKENZIE, A.M.,
Vicar of St. Helen's, Bishopsgate, and Head Master of Queen Elizabeth's Grammar School, St. Olave's, Southwark.

In Two large Volumes, 8vo., Illustrated with Plates, Price 1*l.* 6s. cloth.

A COMPREHENSIVE HISTORY OF THE WOOLLEN TRADE

From the earliest Records to the present Period, comprising the Woollen and Worsted Manufactures, and the Natural and Commercial History of Sheep, with the various Breeds, and Modes of Management in different Countries.

By JAMES BISCHOFF, Esq.

" Mr. Bischoff's work will be found valuable to all persons interested in the subject."—ATHENÆUM.

" Mr. Bischoff has in these volumes collected a vast mass of curious and valuable information, acceptable to readers of varied tastes, even though quite unconnected with manufactures and trade. We recommend every reader to peruse attentively this meritorious compilation."—TIMES.

In Post 8vo., Price 7s. cloth.

A FAMILIAR EXPLANATION OF
THE NATURE, ADVANTAGES, AND IMPORTANCE OF
ASSURANCES UPON LIVES,

And the various Purposes to which they may be usefully Applied: including also a particular Account of the routine required for Effecting a Policy; and of the different systems of Life Assurance now in use, the Principles, Terms, and Tables of Seventy London Assurance Offices, &c.

By LEWIS POCOCK, F.S.A.

" There are no technicalities in Mr. Pocock's work to prevent its being useful to all; and those, therefore, who are likely to have recourse to Life Insurance will do wisely in consulting this familiar explanation of its nature and advantages."—GLOBE.

New Edition, demy 8vo., Revised throughout, with many additions and corrections, by the Author, and Illustrated with Plates. Price 12s., cloth.

THE NATURE AND PROPERTIES OF THE SUGAR CANE;

With Practical Directions for the Improvement of its Culture, and the Manufacture of its Products. To which is added an additional Chapter on the Manufacture of Sugar from Beet-root.

By GEORGE RICHARDSON PORTER, F.R.S.
Corresponding Member of the Institute of France.

By the same Author,

In Demy 8vo., with 45 Botanical Plates, Price 21s.

THE TROPICAL AGRICULTURIST:

A Practical Treatise on the Cultivation and Management of various Productions suited to Tropical Climates, and capable of advantageous production in our Colonies, &c.

" These two valuable volumes open to colonial residents such a mine of hitherto concealed wealth, that every proprietor, emigrant, or person interested in the success of an emigrant friend, ought to procure a copy as their surest guide to fortune."—SCOTSMAN.

Price 6s. bound in cloth.

CLEMENT'S CUSTOMS GUIDE.

Revised and Corrected up to the time of the closing of the last Session of Parliament.

Also, price 2s. cloth.

CLEMENT'S CUSTOMS POCKET MANUAL.
Made up to the same period.

Gresham Prize Essays.

In 8vo., Price 3s. 6d. in cloth, gilt leaves.

ESSAY ON THE
LIFE AND INSTITUTIONS OF OFFA, KING OF MERCIA,
A.D. 755—794.

By the Rev. HENRY MACKENZIE, M.A.

" A very scholarly composition, displaying much research and information respecting the Anglo-Saxon institutions."—SPECTATOR.

In 1 Volume Post 8vo., Price 5s., neatly bound in cloth.

PRIZE ESSAY, 1840.
THE OBLIGATIONS OF LITERATURE
TO THE
MOTHERS OF ENGLAND.

By CAROLINE A. HALSTED.

" The object of the writer has been to show the services rendered by the mothers of England to religion and the state, and to science and learning generally; and the examples adduced display considerable knowledge and research, and are always happily selected and placed in the most attractive point of view."—BRITANNIA.

In 1 Vol. Demy 8vo., with a Portrait, Price 12s.

THE LIFE OF MARGARET BEAUFORT,
COUNTESS OF RICHMOND AND DERBY,
AND MOTHER OF KING HENRY THE SEVENTH,

Foundress of Christ's and of St. John's College, Oxford;

Being the Historical Memoir for which the Honorary Premium was awarded by the Directors of the Gresham Commemoration, Crosby Hall.

By CAROLINE A. HALSTED, Author of "Investigation," &c.

" This work cannot fail of success. The subject is deeply interesting, and has been hitherto almost unexplored. The style is chaste and correct, and has high claims to popularity wide and permanent. On many topics the authoress has accumulated some valuable historical details from sources which have not hitherto been consulted, and has thus compiled a work which, if not entitled to rank amongst the 'curiosities of literature,' is at least one of the most interesting and instructive books of the season."—ATLAS.

Small 8vo., with highly-finished Plates, 7s. in embossed cloth.

INVESTIGATION;
OR, TRAVELS IN THE BOUDOIR.

By CAROLINE A. HALSTED,
Author of "The Life of Margaret Beaufort," &c. &c.

This is an elegantly-written and highly-instructive work for young people, in which a general knowledge of various interesting topics, connected with every-day life, is presented to the youthful mind in an attractive and amusing form.

Third Edition, in 1 Vol. fcap. 8vo., Price 7s. 6d. cloth boards.

THE LAST OF THE PLANTAGENETS :

An Historical Narrative, illustrating some of the Public Events and Domestic and Ecclesiastical Manners of the Fifteenth and Sixteenth Centuries.

"This is a work that must make its way into a permanent place in our literature. The quaintness of its language, the touching simplicity of its descriptions and dialogues, and the reverential spirit of love which breathes through it, will insure it a welcome reception amongst all readers of refined taste and discernment."—ATLAS.

In small 8vo., beautifully Illustrated, Price 7s. in fancy cloth.

THE PROGRESS OF CREATION,
CONSIDERED WITH REFERENCE TO THE
PRESENT CONDITION OF THE EARTH.

An interesting and useful work for young People.

By MARY ROBERTS, Author of "Annals of My Village," &c. &c.

" We have seldom met with a work, in which instruction and entertainment are more happily blended."—TIMES.

"This beautiful volume forms an instructive collection of striking facts, interspersed with amiable reflections."—SPECTATOR.

Foolscap 8vo., Price 5s. cloth.

MEDICAL GUIDE FOR MOTHERS,

In Pregnancy, Accouchement, Suckling, Weaning, &c., and in most of the important Diseases of Children.

Second Edition, enlarged.

By J. R. HANCORN, Member of the Royal College of Surgeons, &c.

An Abridged Edition, just published, Price 1s.

ILLUSTRATED WORKS.

Price 21s., Elegantly Bound,
Forming a splendid Ornament for the Drawing-Room Table.

THE BYRON GALLERY :

A series of 36 Historical Embellishments, illustrating the Poetical Works of Lord Byron; beautifully engraved from original Drawings and Paintings by Sir Thomas Lawrence, P.R.A., H. Howard, R.A., A. E. Chalon, R.A., J. Stothard, R.A., R. Westall, R.A., and other eminent Artists; adapted by their size and excellence to bind up with and embellish every edition published in England of LORD BYRON'S WORKS, and also the various sizes and editions published in France, Germany, and America.

" Adequately to describe the delicate beauty of these splendid plates does not appear to lie within the power of language. There is not an admirer of the works of the departed noble poet who can feel satisfied that he has a perfect edition of them, unless the 'Byron Gallery' be attached to it. There is no instance in which excellence in poetry and the arts are so admirably combined."—IMPERIAL MAGAZINE.

ILLUSTRATED WORKS.

Dedicated, by Permission, to Her Majesty.

Elegantly bound in large Folio.   Price 2*l.* 2*s.*

THE ORIENTAL PORTFOLIO:

A Series of splendid Illustrations of the Scenery, Antiquities, Architecture, Manners, Costumes, &c. of the East. From original Sketches in the collections of Lord William Bentinck, K.C.B., Captain R. M. Grindlay, Lady Wilmot Horton, Sir Henry Willock, K.L.S., Thomas Bacon, Esq., James Baillie Fraser, Esq., and other travellers. The Literary department of the work by HORACE H. WILSON, Esq., M.A., F.R.S., &c. &c.

The object of this undertaking is to supply what has long been felt to be a desideratum; namely, Graphic Illustrations of the Scenery, Antiquities, Architecture, Manners, Costumes, &c. of the East, which, as the theatre of so many brilliant military achievements, and such extensive commercial enterprize, is daily increasing in interest with the British Public.

The Drawings for the Work are made by the First Artists in the Kingdom, from the original sketches taken on the spot. The series is now completed, comprising eleven beautifully finished Plates, tinted in imitation of Drawings.

IMPORTANT SCIENTIFIC WORKS.

In 2 Vols. 8vo., Price 30s. bound in cloth.

'RESEARCHES, PHYSIOLOGICAL AND ANATOMICAL.

By JOHN DAVY, M.D., F.R.S., &c.

Illustrated by numerous Engravings.

The principal subjects treated of are Animal Electricity; — Animal Heat; — the Temperature of different Animals; — Pneumothorax in connexion with the Absorption of Gases by Serous and Mucous Membranes; — the Properties of the Blood in Health and Disease — the Properties of different Animal Textures; — the Putrefactive Process; — the Preservation of Anatomical Preparations; — the Effects of the Poison of certain Serpents; — the Structure of the Heart of Batrachian Animals, &c. &c.

"The subjects treated by the author are extremely numerous and interesting; several new facts in the physiology of animals are brought forward, and some curious and instructive experiments are explained and illustrated with remarkable felicity."—MONTHLY CHRONICLE.

"This work is written with a clearness and simplicity which renders its scientific details readily comprehensible."—HERALD.

IMPORTANT SCIENTIFIC WORKS.

*The only Complete and Uniform Edition of the Works of
Sir Humphry Davy.*

THE LIFE AND COLLECTED

WORKS OF SIR HUMPHRY DAVY, BART.

Foreign Associate of the Institute of France, &c.

Edited by his Brother, JOHN DAVY, M.D., F.R.S.

Now complete, in 9 Vols. Post 8vo., Price 10s. 6d. each in cloth binding.

Contents of the Volumes;—Sold separately.

VOL. I.

THE LIFE OF SIR H. DAVY, WITH A PORTRAIT.

"This biography is admirably written—correct details, full of instruction,
and amusing throughout."—LONDON REVIEW.

VOL. II.

THE WHOLE OF SIR H. DAVY'S EARLY MISCELLANEOUS PAPERS, FROM 1799 to 1805;

With an Introductory Lecture, and Outlines of Lectures on Chemistry
delivered in 1802 and 1804.

VOL. III.

RESEARCHES ON NITROUS OXIDE,

And the Combination of Oxygen and Azote; and on the Respiration of
Nitrous Oxide and other Gases.

VOL. IV.

ELEMENTS OF CHEMICAL PHILOSOPHY.

With Twelve Plates of Chemical Apparatus.

VOLS. V. AND VI.

BAKERIAN LECTURES,

And other Papers in Philosophical Transactions, and Journal of the
Royal Institution. With numerous Engravings.

VOLS. VII. AND VIII.

ELEMENTS OF AGRICULTURAL CHEMISTRY.

Discourses delivered before the Royal Society, Miscellaneous Lectures, and
Extracts from Lectures. With many Plates.

VOL. IX.

SALMONIA, AND CONSOLATION IN TRAVEL.

** This new and uniform edition of the Writings of Sir Humphry
Davy embraces the *whole of his Works,* during the space of thirty years
(1799 to 1829), a period memorable in the History of Chemistry, and
made so, in no small degree, by his own Discoveries.

IMPORTANT SCIENTIFIC WORKS.

, *In order to secure to science the full advantage of Discoveries in Natural History, the Lords Commissioners of Her Majesty's Treasury have been pleased to make a liberal grant of money towards defraying part of the expenses of the following important publications. They have, in consequence, been undertaken on a scale worthy of the high patronage thus received, and are offered to the public at a much lower price than would otherwise have been possible.*

1.

By the Authority of the Lords Commissioners of the Admiralty.

Now Publishing in Royal Quarto Parts, Price 10s. each, with beautifully Coloured Plates.

THE ZOOLOGY OF THE VOYAGE OF H.M.S. SULPHUR,

Under the Command of

CAPTAIN SIR EDWARD BELCHER, R.N., C.B., F.R.G.S., &c.

Edited and Superintended by RICHARD BRINSLEY HINDS, Esq., Surgeon, R.N., attached to the Expedition.

The extensive and protracted Voyage of Her Majesty's Ship "Sulphur," having been productive of many new and valuable additions to Natural History, a number of which are of considerable scientific interest, it has been determined to publish them in a collected form, with illustrations of such as are hitherto new or unfigured. The collection has been assembled from a variety of countries, embraced within the limits of a voyage prosecuted along the shores of North and South America, among the Islands of the Pacific and Indian Oceans, and in the circumnavigation of the globe. In many of these, no doubt, the industry and research of previous navigators may have left no very prominent objects unobserved, yet in others there will for some time remain abundant scope for the Naturalist. Among the countries visited by the "Sulphur," and which in the present state of science are invested with more particular interest, may be mentioned the Californias, Columbia River, the Northwest coast of America, the Feejee Group (a portion of the Friendly Islands,) New Zealand, New Ireland, New Guinea, China, and Madagascar.

Animated by a devotion to science, the following gentlemen have liberally engaged to undertake those departments with which each respectively is best acquainted. The Mammalia will thus be described by Mr. J. E. GRAY; Birds, by Mr. GOULD; Fish, by Dr. RICHARDSON; Crustacea, by Mr. BELL; Shells, by Mr. HINDS; Radiata, by Mr. J. E. GRAY.

PLAN OF PUBLICATION.

I. The work will extend to about *Twelve Parts*, one of which will appear on the 1st of every third month.

II. The Parts will be published at the uniform price of *Ten Shillings*, and it is intended that each department shall, as far as possible, be complete in itself.

, Six Parts of this Work are now published, Parts 1 and 2 containing Mammalia, by Mr. J. E. Gray, and Parts 3 and 4, Birds, by Mr. Gould; Part 5, Ichthyology, by Dr. Richardson; Part 6, Mollusca, by Mr. R. B. Hinds.

IMPORTANT SCIENTIFIC WORKS.

2.

Uniform with the preceding,

In Royal 4to. Parts, Price 10s. and 12s. each, containing on an average Ten beautifully Coloured Engravings, with descriptive Letterpress.

ILLUSTRATIONS OF

THE ZOOLOGY OF SOUTH AFRICA:

Comprising Figures of all the new species of Quadrupeds, Birds, Reptiles, and Fishes, obtained during the Expedition fitted out by "The Cape of Good Hope Association for exploring Central Africa," in the years 1834, 1835, and 1836, with Letterpress Descriptions, and a Summary of African Zoology.

By ANDREW SMITH, M.D.,
Surgeon to the Forces, and Director of the Expedition.

. The whole of the Plates are engraved in the highest style of Art, from the Original Drawings taken expressly for this work, and beautifully coloured after Nature.

20 Parts are now published.

With the Approval of the Lords Commissioners of Her Majesty's Treasury.

GEOLOGICAL OBSERVATIONS

MADE DURING THE VOYAGE OF HER MAJESTY'S SHIP BEAGLE,
Under the Command of Captain Fitzroy, R.N.

PART I.—(JUST PUBLISHED) ON CORAL FORMATIONS.
By CHARLES DARWIN, M.A., F.R.S., Sec. G.S., &c.

In 1 Vol. 8vo., Illustrated with Plates and Wood-cuts, Price 15s. bound in cloth.

PART II.—ON THE VOLCANIC ISLANDS OF THE ATLANTIC AND PACIFIC OCEANS,

Together with a brief Notice of the Geology of the Cape of Good Hope and of part of Australia, price 10s. 6d. Demy 8vo. cloth, with Map.

Preparing for Publication, Demy 8vo., Illustrated with Map, Price 10s. 6d. cloth.

PART III.—ON THE GEOLOGY OF SOUTH AMERICA.

IMPORTANT SCIENTIFIC WORKS.

3.

THE ZOOLOGY OF THE VOYAGE OF H. M. S. BEAGLE,
UNDER THE COMMAND OF CAPTAIN FITZROY, R.N.
DURING THE YEARS 1832 TO 1836.

Edited and superintended by CHARLES DARWIN, Esq., M.A. F.R.S. Sec. G.S. Naturalist to the Expedition.

Comprising highly-finished representations of the most novel and interesting objects in Natural History, collected during the voyage of the Beagle, with descriptive Letterpress, and a general Sketch of the Zoology of the Southern Part of South America.

Figures are given of many species of animals hitherto unknown or but imperfectly described, together with an account of their habits, ranges, and places of habitation.

The collections were chiefly made in the provinces bordering on the Rio Plata, in Patagonia, the Falkland Islands, Tierra del Fuego, Chili, and the Galapagos Archipelago in the Pacific.

THIS WORK IS NOW COMPLETE,

And may be had in sewed Parts, Price 8*l.* 15*s.*, or in half russia or cloth binding, at a small addition to the price.

Nos. 1, 7, 8, and 13,
FOSSIL MAMMALIA.
By Richard Owen, Esq., F.R.S.,
Professor of Anatomy and Physiology to the Royal College of Surgeons, London.

With a Geological Introduction.

By Charles Darwin, Esq., M.A., F.R.S., V.P.G.S.

This Division of the Work complete, Price 1*l.* 10s.

Nos. 2, 4, 5, and 10.
MAMMALIA.
By George R. Waterhouse, Esq.
Curator of the Zoological Society of London, &c.

This Division of the Work complete, Price 1*l.* 18s.

Nos. 3, 6, 9, 11, and 15.
BIRDS.
By John Gould, Esq., F.L.S.
With a Notice of their Habits and Ranges,
By Charles Darwin, Esq., M.A., V.P.G.S., F.R.S.
This Division of the Work complete, Price 2*l.* 15s.

Nos. 12, 14, 16, and 17.
FISH.
By the Rev. Leonard Jenyns, M.A., F.R.S.
This Division of the Work complete, Price 1*l.* 14s.

No. 18, 19.
REPTILES.
By Thos. Bell, Esq., F.R.S. F.L.S., &c. Professor of Geology, King's College.
This Division of the Work complete, Price 18s.

IMPORTANT SCIENTIFIC WORKS.

4.

Uniform with the preceding.

THE BOTANY OF THE VOYAGE OF H.M.S. SULPHUR.

Under the Command of

CAPTAIN SIR EDWARD BELCHER, R.N., C.B., F.R.G.S., &c.,

During the Years 1836-42.

Published under the Authority of the Lords Commissioners
of the Admiralty.

Edited and Superintended by RICHARD BRINSLEY HINDS, Esq.,
Surgeon, R.N., attached to the Expedition.

The Botanical Descriptions by GEORGE BENTHAM, Esq.

Parts I., II., III. and IV. are now ready, price 10s. each, and Part V.
will be Published on the 1st of January.

In one volume, royal 4to., illustrated with 59 beautifully coloured plates,
price 63s., cloth.

ILLUSTRATIONS OF THE RECENT CONCHOLOGY OF GREAT BRITAIN AND IRELAND;

With the Description and Localities of all the Species,—Marine, Land,
and Fresh Water. Drawn and Coloured from Nature.

By CAPTAIN THOMAS BROWN, F.L.S., M.W.S., M.K.S.
Member of the Manchester Geological Society.

HISTORY, TRAVELS, BIOGRAPHY, ETC.

In 1 Vol., demy 8vo., with a New Map by Arrowsmith, Plans of the
Harbour, and numerous Engravings, Price 14s.

A HISTORY OF UPPER AND LOWER CALIFORNIA,

From their first Discovery to the Present Time; comprising an Account
of the Climate, Soil, Natural Productions, Agriculture, Commerce, &c.;
a full View of the Missionary Establishments, and condition of the Free
and Domesticated Indians.

By ALEXANDER FORBES, Esq.

With an Appendix relating to Steam Navigation in the Pacific.

"This is a very interesting and important work, and will make the public
well acquainted with an extensive country known to Europe nearly three
hundred years, yet its history, till the appearance of this volume, has been
nearly a blank."—SUNDAY TIMES.

HISTORY, TRAVELS, BIOGRAPHY, ETC.

In 1 Vol. 8vo., Price 14s. cloth.

A HISTORY OF THE

RUSSIAN CAMPAIGN OF 1814 IN FRANCE.

Translated from the Original of A. MIKHAILOFSK-DANILEFSKY, Aide-de-Camp and Private Secretary of the late Emperor Alexander.

Illustrated by Plans of the Operations of the Army, and of the Seat of War.

"A work of this description, which contributes new data for the Military History of the age, cannot fail of proving acceptable to the public. It is written by a well-known Russian-General; and the details, we feel sure, are as correct as they are interesting."—UNITED SERVICE GAZ.

"Although the military operations of the invasion of France have been before narrated by numerous eye-witnesses, still there is much new and interesting matter in the present history."—NAVAL AND MILITARY GAZ.

In 2 Vols., Post 8vo., with a New Map of the Chinese Empire, Price 1l. 4s. cloth boards.

CHINA OPENED;

Or, a Display of the Topography, History, Customs, Manners, Arts, Manufactures, Commerce, Literature, Religion, Jurisprudence, &c. of the Chinese Empire.

By the Rev. CHARLES GUTZLAFF.

Revised by the Rev. ANDREW REED, D.D.

"We obtain from these volumes more information of a practical kind than from any other publication; a closer view of the domestic life of the Chinese —of the public institutions—the manufactures—natural resources—and literature. The work in fact is full of information, gathered with diligence, and fairly leaves the English reader without any excuse for ignorance on the subject."—ATLAS.

"This is by far the most interesting, complete, and valuable account of the Chinese Empire, that has yet been published."—SUN.

Also by the same Author,

In 2 Vols., Demy 8vo., boards, Price 21s.

A HISTORY OF

THE CHINESE EMPIRE, ANCIENT AND MODERN.

Comprising a Retrospect of the Foreign Intercourse and Trade with China.

Illustrated by a New and Corrected Map of the Empire.

"We cordially recommend this exceedingly interesting account of this very interesting country."—LONDON REVIEW.

"Mr. Gutzlaff has evidently combined industry with talent in producing this work, which far exceeds in information, research, and apparent veracity, any thing we have before seen concerning this curious and singular nation."—LONDON NEWS.

JUVENILE WORKS.

In 6 neatly bound Volumes, Price 3s. 6d. each.

A Valuable and Instructive Present for the Young.

THE PARENTS' CABINET

OF AMUSEMENT AND INSTRUCTION.

Each volume of this useful and instructive little work comprises a variety of information on different subjects—Natural History, Biography, Travels, &c.; Tales, original and selected; and animated Conversations on the objects that daily surround young people.

The various tales and subjects are illustrated with Woodcuts. Each volume is complete in itself, and may be purchased separately.

"Every parent, at all interested in his children, must have felt the difficulty of providing suitable reading for them in their hours of amusement. This little work presents these advantages in a considerable degree, as it contains just that description of reading which will be beneficial to young children."—QUARTERLY JOURNAL OF EDUCATION.

By the same Author,

Royal 18mo., Price 2s. 6d, neatly bound in cloth.

LITTLE STORIES FROM

THE PARLOUR PRINTING-PRESS.

"A very nice little book for children. The author has evidently been familiar with children, and brought himself to understand their feelings. No child's book that we have ever seen has been so admirably levelled at their capacities as this admirably written little book."—WEEKLY CHRONICLE.

Foolscap 8vo., Price 6s. cloth.

THE JUVENILE MISCELLANY

OF AMUSEMENT AND INSTRUCTION.

Illustrated by numerous Plates and Wood Cuts.

"Filled with amusement and instruction as its title indicates."
                                            COURT JOURNAL.

THEOLOGICAL WORKS.

Twelfth Edition, enlarged, with an illustrative Plate, Price 6s. neatly bound
in cloth; or 9s. elegantly bound in morocco.

THE RECTORY OF VALEHEAD,

OR, THE EDIFICE OF A HOLY HOME.

By the Rev. ROBERT WILSON EVANS, M.A.

"Universally and cordially do we recommend this delightful volume.
We believe no person could read this work and not be the better for its pious
and touching lessons. It is a page taken from the book of life, and eloquent
with all the instruction of an excellent pattern : it is a commentary on the
affectionate warning, 'Remember thy Creator in the days of thy youth.'
We have not for some time seen a work we could so deservedly praise, or
so conscientiously recommend."—LITERARY GAZETTE.

The Second Edition, enlarged.   Foolscap 8vo., Price 6s. cloth.

THE RELIGIOUS HISTORY OF MAN,

In which Religion and Superstition are traced from their Source.

By D. MORISON.

How much the contents of this volume call for the careful investigation
of every one in search of Truth, will appear from the following opinions
selected from many.

"The intention of this book is not less admirable than the manner in which
it is written. It is most instructive, and the tone of its contents is in the
highest degree pious, without the least tinge of puritanism. The information
it gives on the most difficult points of biblical reading render it a valuable
book to all who desire true knowledge."—AGE.

"Curious, industrious, and learned, and well worthy the attention of the
public."—LITERARY GAZETTE.

"The plan of this book was both extensive and important—embracing an
inquiry into the nature of Revelation, and its influence on the opinions and
customs of mankind;" BUT "the writer uses *Scripture* as an interpreter,"
and "sticks to the literal text of the six days."—SPECTATOR.

Just published, foolscap 8vo. with an Illustration, price 4s. 6d. cloth.

SCHISM AND REPENTANCE;

A SUBJECT IN SEASON.

By JOSEPH FEARN,

Author of "Belief and Unbelief, a Tale for the Sceptical."

THEOLOGICAL WORKS.

Just Published, Third Edition, Price 12s., 8vo. cloth,

PHILOSOPHY AND RELIGION,

CONSIDERED IN THEIR MUTUAL BEARINGS.

By the Rev. WILLIAM BROWN GALLOWAY, M.A.

Also, recently Published. By the same Author,

In fcap. 8vo., Price 5s., cloth.

THE VOW OF THE GILEADITE:

A LYRIC NARRATIVE.

In 1 Vol., post 8vo., Price 8s. cloth.

THE CHRISTIAN'S SUNDAY COMPANION;

Being Reflections in Prose and Verse on the Collect, Epistle and Gospel, and Proper Lessons for each Sunday; with a view to their immediate connection.

By MRS. J. A. SARGANT.

"We cordially recommend this volume as an acceptable present to be made to the heads of families, and also an admirable school book to be read on Sunday morning to scholars before proceeding to the Temple of God."
CHURCH AND STATE GAZETTE.

"The whole production is eminently fitted to elevate the tone of religious feeling, to strengthen in the minds not only of the rising generation, but also of the older friends to our venerable ecclesiastical institution, sentiments of firm and fervent attachment to the pure faith and reformed worship established in this Protestant country, and for these reasons especially we recommend it to the perusal of our readers."—NORFOLK CHRON.

Sixth Edition, Royal 18mo.,
Price 2s. 6d., handsomely bound in cloth.

LETTERS FROM A MOTHER TO HER DAUGHTER,

AT, OR GOING TO, SCHOOL.

Pointing out the duties towards her Maker, her Governess, her School-fellows, and herself.

By MRS. J. A. SARGANT.

THEOLOGICAL WORKS.

~~~~~~~

In 1 Vol. post 8vo., Price 8s. 6d. neatly bound in cloth.

A HISTORY OF THE CHURCH OF CHRIST,
IN A COURSE OF LECTURES.

By the REV. CHARLES MACKENZIE, A.M.,

Vicar of St. Helen's, Bishopsgate, and Head Master of Queen Elizabeth's
Grammar School, St. Olave's, Southwark.

"Although the author is able and earnest, he is not bigoted or intolerant."
LITERARY GAZETTE.

" It is but an octavo, yet within its conveniently compendious pages it
contains a review carefully taken of the progress of the Church of Christ,
through all the perils of persecution, dissent, and heresy, by which it has
been tried, as in a furnace, up to its confirmed establishment in this country
at the epoch of 1688."—MORNING HERALD.

~~~~~~~

In 1 Vol. small 8vo., Price 7s. cloth boards.

THE LIFE-BOOK OF A LABOURER.

By a WORKING CLERGYMAN.

CONTENTS :—The King's Heart—Links of the Past—Newnham Paddex
and Mr. Blunt—The Grave of Byron—The late Lady Howe—A Fastidious
Parish—Bishops and their Relatives—Lord Viscount Brome—M. J. J.—
Laud's Church Yard—The Rough Clergyman—The Tennis Ball of Fortune
— The Dying Request of the Infidel's Daughter — The Clergyman Alche-
mist—What say you to a Ghost Story?—Lady Huntingdon's resting Place
— Arnsby and Robert Hall — The Deserted Prophetess — The Crown
Prince—Religion and Insanity—Dr. Hawker and Mrs. Jordan, &c. &c.

" It is the pious offering of one who may be deemed a proper follower
in the footsteps of that good man, Legh Richmond."—ARGUS.

" This volume reminds us forcibly of that most delightful of all biographies, ' The Doctor,' to which indeed it is little if at all inferior."
BRITANNIA.

THEOLOGICAL WORKS.

A BOOK FOR THE BEREAVED, AND CONSOLATION FOR THE MOURNER.

In one thick vol. 8vo., price 15s.

MORTAL LIFE;

AND THE STATE OF THE SOUL AFTER DEATH; CONFORMABLE TO DIVINE REVELATION.

By ALEXANDER COPLAND, Esq.

Author of "The Existence of other Worlds," &c.

"This able work will afford in perusal, to all surviving relations, consolation and diversion of mind of the most congenial kind. It neither leads the thoughts to dwell painfully on one idea—that of loss—nor does it altogether withdraw the mind from its contemplation: an effort still more painful. The study of a work like this, on the contrary, while it *gradually weans grief from its melancholy occupation*, supplies it with the sweetest and most cheerful of all balm—THE HAPPY CERTAINTY OF REUNION, not after the lapse of vast ages of time, but of the instant term of mortal existence."—THEOLOGICAL REVIEW.

Just published, price 4s., the Sixth Edition of

THE AUTOBIOGRAPHY OF A DISSENTING MINISTER.

"Our own observation has shown us the truth of the statement put forth in this well-written exposure of the tyranny to which the greater portion of Dissenting Ministers are compelled to submit, and the evils which the destruction of the Established Church would bring upon religion."—COURT JOURNAL.

"We warmly recommend this most excellent work to public notice."
BRITISH MAGAZINE.

"This volume is one which strikes us as being likely to make a considerable stir in the religious, high-church, and dissenting world."
LITERARY GAZETTE.

"Their mode of education at the *Dissenting Colleges*, as they are pompously styled, is admirably shown up."—EDINBURGH EVENING POST.

Second Edition, in 1 Vol. 12mo., Price 4s. 6d. cloth

SIX MONTHS OF

A NEWFOUNDLAND MISSIONARY'S JOURNAL.

By the Venerable Archdeacon WIX.

"This is one of the most interesting and affecting volumes we have ever read."—CHRISTIAN REMEMBRANCER.

"We most earnestly recommend this Journal to general notice; it is full of interest."—BRITISH MAGAZINE.

THEOLOGICAL WORKS.

THE CHAPEL, THE CHURCH, AND THE MEETING-HOUSE.

Recently published, in Foolscap 8vo., Price 6s. bound.

THE CHURCH AND DISSENT,

Considered in their practical influence on 'Individuals, Society, the Nation, and Religion.

By EDWARD OSLER, Esq.

"It would be impossible to find, in the whole range of our literature, a work so admirably suited to the present times as this invaluable little volume. The searching test to which the respective systems have been submitted is so complete and convincing, that the work ought to be studied by every Dissenter and Churchman in the Kingdom, particularly at the present religious crisis."—CHRISTIAN REVIEW.

By the same Author.

In 1 Vol. Royal 8vo., Price 4s. cloth boards.

CHURCH AND KING.

COMPRISING

I. THE CHURCH AND DISSENT, considered in their Practical Influence, shewing the Connexion of Constitutional Monarchy with the Church; and the Identity of the Voluntary Principle with Democracy.

II. THE CHURCH ESTABLISHED ON THE BIBLE; or, the Doctrines and Discipline of the Church shewn in the Order and Connexion of the Yearly Services appointed from the Scriptures.

III. THE CATECHISM explained and illustrated. In connexion with these appointed Services.

IV. PSALMS AND HYMNS on the Services and Rites of the Church.

In 1 thick Vol. Demy 8vo., Price 15s. cloth extra.

THE FAMILY SANCTUARY:

A FORM OF DOMESTIC DEVOTION FOR EVERY SABBATH IN THE YEAR;

CONTAINING

The Collect of the Day; a Portion of Scripture;

An original Prayer and Sermon; and the Benediction.

"The excellence of the object to which this work is addressed will be admitted by Christians of every denomination, who profess to believe in the religion of the Bible. IT IS A COMPLETE BOOK OF FAMILY WORSHIP, and may be recommended with confidence to all families who preserve in their household the Christian practice of DOMESTIC DEVOTION."—THEOLOGICAL REVIEW.

THEOLOGICAL WORKS.

In 1 thick Vol. Demy 8vo., Price 10s. 6d. neatly bound in cloth.

SCRIPTURAL STUDIES:

COMPRISING

THE CREATION—THE CHRISTIAN SCHEME—THE INNER SENSE.

By the Rev. WILLIAM HILL TUCKER, M.A.,
Fellow of King's College, Cambridge.

"This is not a work for ordinary readers. The author thinks for himself; and so writes that his readers must think too, or they will not be able to understand him. To the sacred volume, as a revelation from God, he pays uniform and entire deference—and the thoughtful and prayerful reader will soon find that he has not the thinkings of a common-place mind before him."—METHODIST MAGAZINE.

SOCIAL EVILS AND THEIR REMEDY:

A SERIES OF NARRATIVES.

By the Rev. C. B. TAYLER, M.A.

The First Number, entitled "THE MECHANIC," was pronounced to be "One of the most useful and interesting publications that ever issued from the press."

The following are the Contents of the different Numbers,
Price 1s. 6d. each.

II. The Lady and the Lady's Maid.	VI. Live and Let Live; or, the
III. The Pastor of Dronfells.	Manchester Weavers.
IV. The Labourer and his Wife.	VII. The Soldier.
V. The Country Town.	VIII. The Leaside Farm.

Every two consecutive Numbers form a Volume, which may be procured, neatly bound, Price 4s. each.

"The design of Mr. Tayler is praiseworthy; his object being to counteract, by a series of tales illustrative of the power and necessity of religion in the daily and hourly concerns of life, 'the confusion of error with truth in MISS MARTINEAU'S ENTERTAINING STORIES.'"

CHRISTIAN REMEMBRANCER.

BOOKS FOR THE USE OF THE BLIND,

Printed with a very distinct Raised Roman Letter, adapted to their touch.

	£	s.	d.
THE BIBLE, 15 Vols.	8	0	0

** Any Volume separately :—

	s.	d.
Vol. 1, Genesis	10	0
— 2, Exodus and Leviticus	13	0
— 3, Numbers	9	0
— 4, Deuteronomy	7	6
— 5, Joshua, Judges, and Ruth	10	0
— 6, Samuel	11	0
— 7, Kings	11	0
— 8, Chronicles	11	0
— 9, Job, Ezra, and Nehemiah	9	0
— 10, Psalms	13	0
— 11, Proverbs, Ecclesiastes, Song of Solomon and Esther	8	6
— 12, Isaiah	10	6
— 13, Jeremiah and Lamentations	11	0
— 14, Ezekiel	10	0
— 15, Daniel, to the end	11	0

The Four Gospels—Matthew and Luke 5s. 6d. each; John 4s. 6d.; Mark 4s., separately.

The Church of England Catechism	0	1	0
Church of Scotland Shorter Catechism	0	2	6
Selections from Eminent Authors	0	1	6
Selections of Sacred Poetry, with Tunes	0	2	0
Arithmetical Boards	0	10	6
Map of England and Wales	0	2	0
Ruth and James	0	2	6
Report and Statement of Education	0	2	0
Specimens of Printing Type	0	2	6
First Book of Lessons	0	1	0
Second Book of Lessons	0	2	0
A Selection of Æsop's Fables, with Woodcuts	0	2	0
Lessons on Religion and Prayer	0	1	6
Lessons on Natural Religion	0	2	0
The Acts of the Apostles	0	5	6
The Epistles to the Ephesians and Galatians	0	3	0
The New Testament, complete, 4 vols. bound	2	0	0
The Psalms and Paraphrases, 2 vols.	0	16	0
The Morning and Evening Services	0	2	
The History of the Bible	0	2	0
Musical Catechism, with Tunes	0	3	6
English Grammar	0	5	0
Tod's Lectures, vol. 1 and 2, each	0	2	0
Description of London by Chambers	0	3	6
Meditations on the Sacrament	0	4	0

The Blind may now be taught to read with ease and facility not only at School, but by their own friends at home.

SCHOOL BOOKS.

Second Edition, Post 8vo., Price 10s. 6d. boards.

THE ENGLISH MASTER;

OR,

STUDENT'S GUIDE TO REASONING AND COMPOSITION:

Exhibiting an Analytical View of the English Language, of the Human Mind, and of the Principles of fine Writing.

By WILLIAM BANKS, Private Teacher of Composition, Intellectual Philosophy, &c.

"We have examined with care and pleasure this valuable treatise of Mr. Banks, and strenuously recommend the volume as one of all others most fit to put into the hands of every English student."
WEEKLY REVIEW.

Third Edition, Demy 12mo., Price 3s. bound.

A SYSTEM OF ARITHMETIC,

With the Principles of Logarithms. Compiled for Merchant Taylors' School.

By RICHARD FREDERICK CLARKE, Teacher.

"The great object attained in this excellent work is a most judicious abridgment of the labour of teaching and learning every branch of Arithmetic, by rendering the Rules and Explanations so very simple and intelligible, that the study becomes a pleasure, instead of a task, to the youthful pupil."

24mo. 2s. cloth boards.

THE GRAMMARIAN;

OR,

THE ENGLISH WRITER AND SPEAKER'S ASSISTANT:

COMPRISING

SHALL AND WILL

Made easy to Foreigners, with Instances of their Misuse on the part of the Natives of England.

ALSO

SCOTTICISMS,

Designed to correct Improprieties of Speech and Writing.

By JAMES BEATTIE, LL.D.

SCHOOL BOOKS.

12mo., Price 1s. 6d. bound.

A NEW

SPELLING-BOOK OF THE ENGLISH LANGUAGE;

CONTAINING

All the Monosyllables: a copious selection of Polysyllables, carefully arranged and accented; Progressive Lessons, chiefly from the Holy Scriptures; a list of words of various Meanings; a short Bible Catechism; Questions on Scripture History; and School Prayers.

By J. S. MOORE, Master of the Brewers' Company's School.

Recently published in Demy 12mo., Price 5s. bound in cloth.

A BOOK FOR THE COUNTING-HOUSE AND PRIVATE DESK.

ARITHMETIC UNVEILED:

Being a Series of Tables and Rules, whereby most of the calculations in business may be either mentally performed, or so abridged as to save half the time usually employed. To which are annexed a Multiplication Table extended to 200 times 200, and Tables of Interest on an improved plan. The whole adapted to the use of the first merchant and most humble trader.

By JAMES McDOWALL, Accountant.

ORIENTAL PUBLICATIONS.

In 1 Vol., demy 8vo. with Illustrations, price 12s. cloth.

HISTORICAL RECORD OF

The Honourable East India Company's

FIRST MADRAS EUROPEAN REGIMENT;

Containing an Account of the Establishment of Independent Companies in 1645, their formation into a Regiment in 1748, and its subsequent Services to 1842.

ORIENTAL PUBLICATIONS.

In 1 Vol., Post 8vo., Price 9s. cloth lettered.

THE MANNERS AND CUSTOMS OF SOCIETY IN INDIA;

Including Scenes at the Mofussil Stations, interspersed with Characteristic
Tales and Anecdotes: to which is added

A GUIDE TO CADETS

And other Young Gentlemen, during their first Years' Residence in India.

By Mrs. Major CLEMONS.

" We need not recommend this book; the space we have given to it is an
ample proof of the pleasure we have enjoyed in its perusal. We earnestly
advise every person interested in India to read it."—ATLAS.

POETRY.

Just published, royal 18mo., price 4s., cloth gilt.

GRISELDA;

A Dramatic Poem,

Translated from the German of FREDERICK HALM.

By Q. E. D.

" An elegant translation of an elegant German Poem."—ATHENÆUM.

" In conclusion, we would strongly recommend 'Griselda' to our readers;
assuring them that, in our opinion, they will not easily meet with anything
so deserving of popularity, either from the purity of the style, the interest of
the story, the fidelity of the translation, the easy flow of the ryhme, or the ele-
gance of the language."—FOREIGN AND COLONIAL QUARTERLY REVIEW.

Just Published, in Demy 8vo., Price 10s., handsomely bound in cloth.

THE COLUMBIAD.

A Poem in Four Parts.

By ARCHIBALD TUCKER RITCHIE, Esq.

Comprising geographical sketches and a narrative of nautical adven-
tures in the Eastern Seas, including the perils of a storm, and provi-
dential escape from shipwreck; with meditations on a future state.

POETRY.

Just Published, in Demy 8vo., Price 6s. bound.

DAYS IN THE EAST.

A Poem in two Cantos, descriptive of Scenery in India, the departure from Home, the Voyage, and subsequent Career of an Officer in the East India Company's Army.

By JAMES HENRY BURKE, Esq., of Marble Hill;

Lieutenant Bombay Engineers; Member of the Bombay Branch Royal Asiatic Society.

" The stanzas of Mr. Burke bespeak at once high feeling, a vigorous cultivated intelligence, and delicate poetic taste."—MORNING HERALD.

In post 8vo, in sewed cover, price 2s. 6d.

THE ANGLO-INDIAN AND COLONIAL ALMANACK,

AND

CIVIL, MILITARY, AND COMMERCIAL

DIRECTORY

FOR 1845.

The HOME DEPARTMENT of the Almanack will comprise—I. CIVIL and ECCLESIASTICAL; including the Government offices and the India House; together with the forms of procedure, and educational studies, requisite for obtaining civil appointments, and all matters connected with those appointments, from the commencing salary to the retiring allowance. II. MILITARY and MARINE; including information of a similar kind respecting these services, and the Home Establishment of the East India Company. III. COMMERCIAL; containing lists of Merchants, Agents, Associations, &c., throughout the United Kingdom; likewise the trades connected with India and the Colonies; and tariff of Indian and colonial produce.

The EAST INDIAN AND COLONIAL DEPARTMENT will embrace— I. CIVIL: The Government Lists of Bengal, Madras, Bombay, Ceylon, Hong Kong, Australia, New Zealand, Mauritius, and the Cape of Good Hope; lists of Civil Servants and their appointments, and of Judicial Establishments, with a detailed account of the Benefit Funds. II. MILITARY: Staff and Field Officers; distribution of the Army, including the Royal Troops; Ecclesiastical Establishment; and all Benefit Funds. III. COMMERCIAL: List of Mercantile Firms, Banks, Insurance Companies, Public Institutions, &c., in India and the Colonies; with the respective Tariffs, and Tables of Money, Weights, Measures, &c., and other miscellaneous information.

London: Printed by STEWART and MURRAY, Old Bailey.

28

Milton Keynes UK
Ingram Content Group UK Ltd.
UKHW020740280424
441851UK00005B/96